Diane Marie Howard

"*Mixed Ministry* is nutrition for the mind. While directed specifically at church staff relationships, Sue, Kelley, and Henry describe healthful thinking patterns for Christian men and women wherever they work together. Christian men every   t the distortions unconsciously abs   1 society. Like a nightingale singing   s up a sweet melody to carry your C   1 they make me king, I will require t.

—Dr. Michael S. Lawson
Senior Professor and Chairman, Christian Education Department
Dallas Theological Seminary

"*Mixed Ministry* is an important book for anyone in church leadership to read. It offers practical guidance, surprisingly refreshing examples, and great discussion topics for people who are serious about serving the Lord long-term."

—Dr. Sarah Sumner
Author, *Men and Women in the Church*

"This book opens the closet, revealing the tug-of-war between hurting women and men in ministry. . . . The authors' perspectives are real, relevant, and reconciling."

—Dr. Sheila M. Bailey
President, E. K. Bailey Ministries, Inc.
Dallas, TX

"*Mixed Ministry* shows the true value of the unique differences of men and women working together in ministries. It also points out the pitfalls and how to avoid them. We have missed so many opportunities over the years because of wrong perceptions and stereotypes. Men and women have very different insights and strengths that are missed if we ignore or overlook them."

—Arch Bonnema
Producer, *The Genius Club*
CEO, Joshua Financial, Plano, TX

"This is a book for the twenty-first century! As the church moves forward spreading the love of Christ, it must do so in an atmosphere of partnership and celebration. Because men and women are created in God's image, we must find a way to work together to build his kingdom. *Mixed Ministry* shows us the way! Through personal stories, historical and biblical examples, research findings, and challenging discussion questions, the reader becomes equipped and energized to do the work God has called us to do together, as brothers and sisters in the family of God."

—DR. CYNTHIA FANTASIA
Pastor of Women, Grace Chapel
Lexington, MA

"One of the greatest challenges many women in ministry face is . . . working on a predominately male staff, faculty, or team. Finally we have a healthy perspective with which to find and maintain our equilibrium. . . . [*Mixed Ministry*] brings promise of expanded kingdom work by men and women working alongside one another as beloved brothers and sisters, the kind of relationships exemplified by Paul and Jesus."

—DR. BEV HISLOP
Assistant Professor of Pastoral Care to Women
Executive Director, Women's Center for Ministry
Western Seminary, Portland, OR

"Sue, Kelley, and Henry have surfaced a significant shortcoming that is often overlooked in most organizations. Healthy partnerships between men and women coworkers are critical to success, and this book definitely tackles the subject head-on!"

—NORM MILLER
Chairman of the Board, Interstate Battery System of America
Dallas, TX

"For too long women have been marginalized and men have been burdened with excessive responsibilities. This book exposes one of the main causes of weak, unhealthy Christian ministry: the failure to recognize the value God places on men and women serving together in leadership as brothers and sisters. As each learns to appreciate the unique contribution of the other, the body of Christ will grow stronger and will more accurately reflect the love and unity of God to the world."

—DR. JOYE BAKER
Adjunct Professor, Dallas Theological Seminary

"Here are answers—courageous, biblical, and eminently practical solutions—to furtive questions about improper relationships. A book begging to be written, this realistic discussion invades our increasingly unmanageable fantasyland where men-women ministry teams often flirt with disaster in disguise. Single or married, everyone who works with the opposite sex needs to read and ponder this excellent heads-up manual on how to stay out of sexual sinkholes."

—DR. HOWARD G. HENDRICKS
Chairman, Center for Christian Leadership
Distinguished Professor, Dallas Theological Seminary

MIXED MINISTRY

WORKING TOGETHER
AS BROTHERS AND SISTERS
IN AN OVERSEXED SOCIETY

Sue Edwards | Kelley Mathews | Henry J. Rogers

Kregel
Academic & Professional

Be grateful for doors of opportunity
and for friends who oil the hinges.

To Lesa Engelthaler,
Eva Bleeker, and Luke Kavlie,
who oiled the hinges
by contributing their time, words, and ideas
to the concepts on these pages.

Contents

Acknowledgments

"A MAN GAVE A WOMAN HIS seat on the bus; she fainted. When she revived, she thanked him, and he fainted." This little quip seems to say that women are surprised when men come to their aid and men are shocked at their gratitude. Stereotypes can be so wrong! To our delight, both men and women responded quickly and enthusiastically to our requests for help, living out the premise of this book—that we are brothers and sisters in Christ. Lesa Engelthaler and Eva Bleeker met with us weekly over a summer to wrestle with words and concepts, lending us their writing expertise. Our amazing research assistant, Luke Kavlie, scoured libraries and the Internet on behalf of the project. Jay Quine steered us in a positive direction with his excellent advice. Every generation was represented on the team.

Prominent leaders made room for us in their busy schedules, cheering us on. Thanks to Howard Hendricks, John Ortberg, Bill Hybels, Dan Allender, Ronna Miller, Mike Lawson, Frank James, Steve Roese, Andy McQuitty, Elizabeth Maring, Jay Quine, Jim Thames, Mark Heinemann, and Scott Stonehouse, as well as students, lay leaders, colleagues, and friends who gave us input through surveys and discussions. We are indebted to many of these leaders' administrative assistants who, when they heard about the nature of our work, procured their bosses' attention. You work behind the scenes but the Lord knows who you are, and we thank you. A special thanks to Kelly Arabie for her early encouragement and help with rough drafts.

We are grateful for our friends at Kregel—Dennis Hillman, Miranda Gardner, Amy Stephansen, Leslie Paladino, and our fantastic editor Wendy Widder. You gave us a platform for our message, guiding us with integrity and professionalism. We sense that your work is more than business—it's a ministry, making our partnership a pleasure.

We also want to acknowledge the support and encouragement of our spouses, David Edwards, John Mathews, and Kathy Rogers. For your sacrifices so we could work, this book is yours too.

To our readers, we hope this book tweaks your thinking and behavior toward your sacred siblings. Thanks for investing the time to investigate this ignored subject. May our Lord use this book to help us all walk in pure attitudes and actions, but most of all to strengthen our mixed-gender partnerships for his glory.

Contributors

Dr. Dan B. Allender received his M.Div. from Westminster Theological Seminary and his Ph.D. in counseling psychology from Michigan State University. He taught at Grace Theological Seminary for seven years (1983–1989). From 1989–1997, Dan worked as a professor in the Master of Arts in Biblical Counseling program at Colorado Christian University, Denver, Colorado. Currently, he serves as president and professor of counseling at Mars Hill Graduate School, Seattle, Washington. He travels and speaks extensively to present his unique perspective on sexual abuse recovery; love and forgiveness; worship; and other related topics. Dan is the author of a number of books, including *The Wounded Heart*, *The Healing Path*, *How Children Raise Parents*, *Leading with a Limp*, and *To Be Told*, and has coauthored several books with Dr. Tremper Longman, including *Intimate Allies*, *The Cry of the Soul*, *Bold Love*, and *Breaking the Idols of Your Heart*.

Eva Bleeker and her husband, Josh, make their home in the Dallas metro area, but she is a Kansas farm girl at heart. Eva graduated from Dallas Theological Seminary with an M.A. in media and communications and an M.A. in Christian education. Eva gains her greatest joys from teaching the Bible to women, writing, and ministering through music.

Lesa Engelthaler is a freelance writer whose work has been published in the *Dallas Morning News, Leadership Journal, Kindred Spirit*, and *Discipleship Journal*. As a young woman, Lesa had the privilege of being mentored by several women. Realizing the potential reservoir of experience that older women extend to younger leaders, Lesa founded a mentoring program for her church. In the past nine years, more than 180 women of all ages have graduated from the program. In recent years Lesa has led a team of speakers and counselors at women's conferences in rural southern Mexico. Lesa is also a senior associate for the Dallas-based executive search firm TNS Partners, assisting nonprofit organizations in identifying and recruiting senior leaders.

Dr. Howard Hendricks serves as distinguished professor and chair of the Center for Christian Leadership at Dallas Theological Seminary. He earned his B.A. from Wheaton College (1946); his Th.M. from Dallas Theological Seminary (1950); and his D.D. degree from Wheaton College (1967). Dr. Hendricks is a household name in Christianity, and in his fifty-plus years of ministry, he has directly or indirectly touched millions of lives. A DTS faculty member since 1951, Dr. Hendricks sees the adult children of former students now attending his classes. Today he maintains a rigorous travel schedule and has ministered in more than eighty countries through speaking engagements, radio, books, tapes, and films. He is also the former Bible teacher and chaplain for the Dallas Cowboys football team.

Dr. Hendricks's numerous publications include *As Iron Sharpens Iron: Building Character in a Mentoring Relationship* (Moody, 1995); *Living by the Book* (Moody, 1993); *Color Outside the Lines: A Revolutionary Approach to Creative Leadership* (Word, 1998); and *Teaching to Change Lives* (Multnomah, 1987).

Dr. Frank James III is president of Reformed Theological Seminary in Orlando, Florida. He also serves as professor of historical and systematic theology and professor of church history there. He is a graduate of Texas Tech University, and was awarded a D.Phil.

in history from Oxford University (1993) and a Ph.D. in theology from Westminster Theological Seminary in Pennsylvania (2000). Since 1996, he has been general editor of the Peter Martyr Library and senior editor of Ad Fontes: Digital Library of Classical Theological Texts. He is the author of *Peter Martyr Vermigli: Praedestinatio Dei in the Thought of an Italian Reformer* and coeditor of *Via Augustini: Augustine in the Later Middle Ages, Renaissance and Reformation.* In addition, he has published many articles and essays in academic and popular journals.

Dr. Michael Lawson is department chair and senior professor of Christian education at Dallas Theological Seminary. His degrees include: B.B.A., University of North Texas (1965); Th.M., Dallas Theological Seminary (1969); Ph.D., Oklahoma University (1983). Dr. Lawson has a special burden for developing world churches and their Christian education programs. He has devoted eighteen years to DTS and more than three decades to pastoral work and Christian education. He maintains an international teaching schedule to Europe, the former Soviet Union, the Caribbean, Asia, Central America, the Middle East, India, China, and Africa. In addition, Dr. Lawson developed the National Congress on Christian Education for Mexico City. Tish, his wife of over forty years, serves as his assistant in the Christian Education department.

Dr. Andy McQuitty is a graduate of Wheaton College, Wheaton, Illinois. He earned his D.Min. degree from Dallas Theological Seminary in 1997, receiving the C. Summer Wemp Award in personal evangelism as well as the John G. Mitchell Award for outstanding scholarship and effectiveness in ministry. Andy has served as a youth pastor in Washington State, and as associate pastor of a Bible church in Garland, Texas. As senior pastor of Irving Bible Church (Irving, Texas) since 1987, he transitioned the church to a contemporary style of ministry with a strong emphasis on world missions and the arts. Under his leadership, IBC has grown from three hundred to four thousand adults in four worship services each Sunday, with extensive children's and youth ministries.

Ronna Miller received her B.A. in business and communication from Whitworth College (Spokane, Washington) and her M.Div. and a Certificate in Spiritual Direction from Mars Hill Graduate School in Seattle, Washington. A speaker and teacher for more than fifteen years in both religious and secular settings, she also serves as a spiritual director, walking alongside others as they travel toward and with God. She is now the director of conferences at MHGS, marketing the institution in provocative and transformative ways around the country through the voices of those who work, teach, write, and lead within the school. She was instrumental in creating the Leadership Crucible (http://www.leadershipcrucible.com), a three-day experiential learning environment that ushers leaders into profound levels of vulnerability, honesty, and growth. Currently working toward the dream of a book, Ronna hopes to challenge women to levels of extravagance, risk, and life that far exceed their wildest dreams.

Steve Roese is excecutive pastor at Irving Bible Church, where he has served for the last ten years. He is a graduate of New York University and Dallas Theological Seminary and is presently working on his D.Min. at Bakke Graduate University. He has been married for almost twenty years and has three teenage children.

Scott Stonehouse is an executive with AT&T and a member of Richland Bible Church in Richardson, Texas.

Part 1

SEEING ONE ANOTHER AS SIBLINGS

Chapter 1

New Eyes

You're my brother, you're my sister,
So take me by the hand.
Together we will work until He comes.
There's no foe that can defeat us
When we're walking side by side.
So long as there is love,
We will stand.

—RUSS TAFF

BILLY CRYSTAL AND MEG RYAN immortalized the popular (mis)understanding of male-female relationships in the hit movie *When Harry Met Sally.*[1] When Harry makes a pass at Sally, his fellow coed, she turns him down with the familiar words, "No, Harry . . . we are just going to be friends, OK?" Harry responds: "Friends! You realize, of course, that we could never be friends." The rest of the conversation proceeds like this:

SALLY: Why not?

HARRY: What I'm saying . . . is that men and women can't be friends because the sex part always gets in the way.

SALLY: That's not true. I have a number of men friends and there is no sex involved.

HARRY: No, you don't.

SALLY: Yes, I do.

HARRY: No, you don't.

SALLY: Yes, I do.

HARRY: You only think you do.

SALLY: Are you saying that I'm having sex with these men without my knowledge?

HARRY: No, I'm saying they all want to have sex with you.

SALLY: No, they don't.

HARRY: Yes, they do . . .

SALLY: How do you know?

HARRY: Because no man can be friends with a woman he finds attractive. He always wants to have sex with her.

Their argument continues, with Harry maintaining that all male-female friendships are doomed because "the sex thing" is "already out there." Sally remains dubious but concludes regretfully, "That's too bad because you are the only person I know in New York."[2]

Poor Sally! What a choice when it comes to men—romance or nothing. Why not "just" friends? Is a pure, nonromantic relationship really impossible between a man and a woman, or is Harry wrong? More specifically, how does Harry's theory relate to men and women who follow Christ? We believe that Christians, indwelt by the Spirit, will prove Harry to be wrong. Men and women really can be friends. In Christ, they can be more than friends—they can be sacred siblings, and the implications for ministry are enormous!

Steve and Sue

"Our women need relevant, in-depth Bible study and I'm willing to do whatever it takes to make that happen." Steve's eyes burned with brotherly passion as he offered me the position of minister-to-women in his church. For seven years, I (Sue) had led the women's ministry in another megachurch where I was never paid a penny even though I sometimes clocked sixty-hour workweeks. Although I was grateful for the opportunity to learn and serve there, I grieved that I had almost no access to the senior pastor, never attended a staff meeting, and felt marginalized in churchwide decisions that affected my ministry.

Steve's offer included everything I needed to create a dynamic, relevant women's ministry, including his full support, my own administrative assistant, a large budget, the chance to join the lead team, a generous salary, and flexible hours. Even more inviting was Steve's brotherly demeanor and his authentic desire to see women of the church mature.

Over the years, I served alongside Steve. The women's Bible study grew from under a hundred to over eight hundred. Diverse women—single, married, widowed, from all ages and walks of life, stay-at-home moms and professional women—met weekly in small groups to study, pray, and process life together. Women in the church implemented evangelistic dinners, retreats, and special interest seminars and ministries, including ones relating to postabortion and infertility. Bible teachers and small group leaders were trained. Women fed families in crisis and reached out to the incarcerated and the poor.

During those years, the church grew in spiritual maturity and numerically, requiring new facilities. As Steve and I toured our new 12 million-dollar building, he commented, "You know, Sue, we could not have done this without your ministry." My heart swelled with gratitude. I thanked God for the opportunity to serve in a place where men and women worked together as brothers and sisters, knowing that this partnership contributed to the success of the whole church and to God's glory.

Kristen and Jason

Kristen was born into a family of speed skaters. She learned to skate at the age of two and competed at four. Her grandfather

flooded his back yard for a skating rink for her to learn to skate and
later took her skating at local rinks. At twenty-three, Kristen's med-
als and accolades crowded the family mantel. Now—to top off a
stellar career—Olympic gold was in her sights. Then her nineteen-
year-old brother, Jason, was diagnosed with aplastic anemia, a rare
and potentially fatal condition that impedes the body's ability to
produce blood cells. His only hope was a bone marrow transplant
and Kristen was the match. Dr. Jones candidly informed her that
the procedure might weaken her and probably end any hope of winning a medal. It did.

In an interview at Johns Hopkins Hospital, Kristen told report-
ers, "Skating is just skating. It's important, but nothing is more important than life. After all, he's my brother."[3] Kristen had a shot at
glory and a 1994 Olympic medal but chose to give her brother life
instead. By the way, Kristen was elected to the Speed Skaters Hall
of Fame in 2004.[4]

Paul and Lynda

Paul and Lynda's friendship grew out of his respect for her professional abilities. "She was disciplined, serious, and capable in
managing document control, which is a key role in an engineering
company," says Paul. "The value of everything you design is in the
documentation and Lynda did a wonderful job of keeping that all
straight." But what began as a friendship based in work-related issues deepened because of Lynda's personal need for Jesus.

They were friends, so Lynda naturally looked to Paul for spiritual
answers. "I started questioning him about Christ and his beliefs. I
wasn't a Christian at the time and Paul became like a mentor to me.
Raili (Paul's wife) and Paul invited me to friendship day at their
church and it went from there."

When asked to describe their relationship, Paul says, "We have
such easy communication. It was exciting to watch as God grew
Lynda, and I could see those changes. I saw the hardness melting
away."

Paul knows the importance of personal relationships, even with

women in the workplace. "I fundamentally believe that the reason
God has put us on this planet is to relate . . . a fundamental part of
God's nature is relating, and we need to reflect that . . . it starts with
respect and trust . . . that is the foundation of our friendship."[5]

■   ■   ■

Steve for Sue, Kristen for Jason, and Paul for Lynda—the former
paved the way for the latter, living out sibling love. Only Kristen and
Jason are biological sister and brother, but the others are not related
by blood. Nevertheless, the others are equally brothers and sisters in
the eyes of God the Father. In the family of God, they are spiritual
brothers and sisters.

This is a book about family—not biological family—but what it
means to *see* one another as brothers and sisters in Christ, the way
God intended. This has ramifications. With new eyes, we can work
together as men and women in a spiritual family, blessing each other
rather than setting one another aside because of gender. This book
will challenge all of us to examine our gender biases and perceptions. This book is for men and women who want to make an impact
for Christ—both those who earn their living in ministry and those
who volunteer a few hours a week.

> Of course men and women can work together as brothers
> and sisters in Christ. This is the biblical perspective, and
> failure to acknowledge this is a denial of the redemptive
> power of Christ's work in our lives. However, this is a fallen
> world and there is such a thing as sibling rivalry. Male-
> female relationships are caught in the "already–not yet"—
> already redeemed, but not yet fully sanctified.
>
> —Dr. Frank James

One Hypercharged Factor

What blinds us from seeing one another as siblings? The answer
is different for each of us. We will wrestle with these complexities

in the following chapters. Sexual temptation is one hypercharged factor we cannot ignore—for both men and women, especially in our oversexed culture. It's almost impossible not to be influenced by women with bare bellies and exposed cleavage, and muscular men sporting steely pecs and abs. God asks each of us to take charge of our hearts and hormones and submit them to Christ for the glory of God and building up of his kingdom.

What Does the Bible Say?

The Bible tells us straight up how we should behave.

> Do not rebuke an older man harshly, but exhort him as if he were your father. Treat younger men as brothers, older women as mothers, and younger women as sisters, with absolute purity. (1 Tim. 5:1–2)

Paul indicates that in the community of faith we are called to honor older, mature men and women as if they were godly parents, and treat male and female peers as if they were our brothers and sisters. Paul insists that we see the opposite sex as family members first, not as sexual objects. God considers lust between a biological brother and sister to be abhorrent (Lev. 20:17). Just as sinful is lust between any man and woman, according to Jesus (Matt. 5:28). Shouldn't it be unthinkable to lust after a spiritual brother or sister? Followers of Jesus are to consider one another as family, as sacred siblings. Is this mission impossible? Are we able to see one another this way in the family of faith? Yes, God enables us through the power of the Holy Spirit working in our hearts and minds to love one another as siblings. How might our churches be changed if men and women caught this vision and lived it out?

Jesus too supports our premise—that with new eyes, Christian men and women can thrive as brothers and sisters in a spiritual family, leading to powerful partnerships in ministry. Yes, Jesus was a family man! Not in the sense that he was married and fathered biological children, but in the sense that he inaugurated the spiritual family we call the church. Consider his response to his mother, Mary, and his biological brothers in this interchange:

> While Jesus was still talking to the crowd, his mother and brothers stood outside, wanting to speak to him. Someone told him, "Your mother and brothers are standing outside, wanting to speak to you." He replied to him, "Who is my mother, and who are my brothers?" Pointing to his disciples, he said, "Here are my mother and my brothers. For whoever does the will of my Father in heaven is my brother and sister and mother." (Matt. 12:46–50)

Undoubtedly Jesus' biological family felt that, as blood kin, they deserved his attention. He should stop what he was doing and come out to see them. Although he loved his mother and brothers, Jesus used this occasion to teach an important truth. He had come to create a new kind of family. Not a family related by genes, common heritage, or shared genealogy. It is a faith family, and in this passage, Jesus reveals that this new spiritual family trumps blood kin.

The Problem

Do Christian men and women see one another as brothers and sisters in a spiritual family? Are they working together in powerful partnerships? Is this an accurate picture of how most men and women relate to one another in the church today? Our interview responses from men and women across the country were mixed on this topic. We sought out men and women known as positive examples of healthy working partnerships in order to draw from their expertise and experiences. Most saw themselves as pioneers and grieved that their healthy experiences of sibling friendships were so rare. Their stories pepper the pages ahead.

Sadly, many others we have interviewed or have counseled through the years reflect the findings in a research project conducted by Dr. Joye Baker at Dallas Theological Seminary in 2004. She surveyed 377 female seminary graduates to identify their most difficult leadership challenges. Their answers to the question, "How can the seminary best prepare women students to meet these challenges?"

■ Prepare men and women to more successfully minister together (24 percent).
■ Help men value and respect women in ministry (18 percent).[6]

Granted, this is a limited sampling and reflects just one seminary, but their responses echo what we hear over and over, from both men and women who believe we are missing critical opportunities to work together. It begins with the way we *see* one another.

Few of us see and treat the opposite sex with sibling love. When was the last time you evaluated your relationships with the opposite sex in this light? When was the last time you heard a message on this topic? We have not been taught to see one another through the eyes of a Christlike sibling. Current problems between men and women in ministry cause us sometimes to resemble a dysfunctional family. This perspective is especially difficult in a culture where sexual images and messages constantly bombard us.

> I think too often churches either avoid the topic or settle for an unbiblical "strategy of isolation" where men deliberately separate themselves from women as a means of temptation avoidance. This leads to a loss of biblical community, lost opportunities for the development of leadership gifts, and doesn't even help in avoiding sin. For God's intent is that we aim at becoming *the kind of persons* who treat one another as brother and sister.
>
> —Dr. John Ortberg[7]

Paying a High Price

Consider the state of the American church. Since 1950, membership in all American denominations, except Southern Baptists, has declined.[8] In the United States, there are 40 million unchurched men and women who call themselves Christians but do not belong to a community of believers.[9] Women comprise 60 percent of American churches, yet there has been a 22 percent slip in women's church attendance since 1991. Women are leaving Christianity for alternative spiritualities by the millions.[10] These statistics indicate that the American church may be headed for serious trouble in the coming decades unless we tackle issues that hinder us. We believe resolution of gender conflict could make a real difference. How might healthy, dynamic teams of brothers and sisters impact the future church in America?

Healthy faith families, just like biological families, need both men's and women's ideas, gifts, and perspectives in order to thrive. Single parents will testify that it's tough being both mom and dad. Children need a mother's tender touch and a father's guidance and protection. But many ministries today are like single parent families. The male presence is strong but the mother's touch is missing, or, in other ministries, the female influence is so dominant that the father's guidance is absent, and that lack skews ministry decisions and effectiveness. Neither is healthy. Throughout this book, we will show how the combination makes ministries more effective, strengthening the future church in America.

The Role of Women in the Church

The hot debate over the role of women in ministry also affects the manner in which godly men and women treat one another. We will not address the issue of the role of women in this book. Whatever your view on women's roles, it does not negate God's command in 1 Timothy 5:1–2 to treat one another as brothers and sisters. Theological matters are sometimes used as smoke screens to hide the real issues that lie within our hearts and minds. Let's look deep into ourselves and be honest. If we refuse to face these issues directly, the cost may be high for ourselves and for God's work. But if we learn to see one another as siblings and work together, we believe much of the wrangling over roles will subside.

Protection from Sexual Temptation

We realize that bringing men and women together in ministry frightens many Christians. They fear that God will be dishonored. We have all seen too many pastors succumb to sexual temptation and destroy their families and ministries in the process.[11] We share this concern. The traditional strategy to avoid this tragedy has been to isolate men and women from one another, but this tactic has not worked. We will argue that healthy sibling love actually *protects* pastors from immorality. We will show you how in the following pages.

> This is my partner in ministry. She just happens to be a woman.
>
> —Dr. Jay Quine[12]

Our Game Plan

We believe that with "new eyes," Christian men and women can create healthy working partnerships. In the pages that follow, we will look at how Jesus treated women with compassion—even women with questionable reputations. We will also explore the brotherly love Paul exhibited toward women ministry partners.

We will offer practical suggestions on how men and women can develop new eyes and how we can work together. What does sibling love look like outside a biological family? How do we relate to sacred siblings in personal conversations, staff meetings, and professional development outings?

We must not ignore safeguards to protect ourselves from sexual misconduct and infidelity—but what are those safeguards? Our interviews with mature men and women leaders may surprise you. In part two of this book, we will tackle some of the issues that can get in the way of healthy sibling relationships. How much intimacy is wise between sacred siblings? How do we deal with what goes on in our heads if we find ourselves sexually attracted to a coworker or friend of the opposite sex? Do we handle all attractions the same? How can we learn to be "safe" siblings with our dress, actions, and communication? What are appropriate bridges and fences? How do we decrease the risk to our marriages while serving alongside a brother or sister in ministry? What role do modesty and pornography play in sibling relationships in the church? How do we include and communicate with our spouses so they are not uncomfortable with our sibling relationships?

Is It Worth the Work to Change?

The Bible shows us sibling love—in the next two chapters we will see how Jesus and Paul model it. But is it that simple? No. We realize this is a complex and thorny subject. We will explore these issues together as male and female authors and pepper our work with the thoughts, wisdom, and experiences of respected male and female scholars, pastors, and theologians. We need the perspectives of both genders in writing, life, and ministry.

Is it worth the effort to change? Change requires hard work. Rethinking the way we relate to the opposite sex is challenging and requires introspection and effort. But we believe the rewards will be worth the effort. We believe that churches will grow both spiritually and numerically when men and women serve together as brothers and sisters.

Hear out our arguments in the subsequent pages. The questions we have raised deserve answers. Until we wrestle with these issues, most of us won't be persuaded that healthy sibling love in ministry will work, regardless of what the Bible says or how Jesus and Paul acted. So wrestle with us, but remember that the Bible speaks clearly, admonishing us to treat one another as brothers and sisters "with absolute purity" (1 Tim. 5:2). If we can figure this out, it just might change ministry ethos, attract unbelievers, and glorify God in the process.

Let's begin by watching Jesus, our brother.

Don't assume women can't contribute. Don't assume they want some kind of relationship with you. But remember that people will first think the worst so try not to give them a chance. Be careful!

—Dr. Jim Thames[13]

DISCUSSION QUESTIONS

1. Do you agree or disagree with Harry's statement to Sally, "Friends? You realize, of course, that we could never be friends." Explain your answer.

2. Have you ever observed a healthy, nonsexual friendship between a man and a woman? If so, describe the relationship.

3. Have you experienced this kind of friendship? If so, what were the benefits? What were the challenges?

4. In your opinion, how does our hypercharged sexual culture impact potential mixed-gender friendships?

5. Jesus describes Christian relationships in family terms in Matthew 12:46–50 and Paul does the same in 1 Timothy 5:1–2. Do men and women see one another as family in your church? What are the ramifications of their perspective?

6. Do you view Christians of the opposite sex through sibling eyes? If not, what attitude changes and action steps might correct your eyesight?

Chapter 2

Not Segregation but Transformation

Dear God, I bet it is very hard for you to love all of everybody in the whole world. There are only four people in our family and I can never do it.

—NAN

A Place for Mary

As Jesus and his disciples were on their way, he came to a village where a woman named Martha opened her home to him. She had a sister called Mary, who sat at the Lord's feet listening to what he said. But Martha was distracted by all the preparations that had to be made. She came to him and asked, "Lord, don't you care that my sister has left me to do the work by myself? Tell her to help me!"

"Martha, Martha," the Lord answered, "you are worried and upset about many things, but only one thing is needed. Mary has chosen what is better, and it will not be taken away from her." (Luke 10:38–42)

Sounds of approaching male voices instantly turned the private space of our home into a public space. *My shawl, where is my shawl?* I scurried from room to room, frenzied and frustrated. Finally, I spied it in a heap in the corner. Quickly I secured it in place. Their conversation grew louder and louder as they rounded the corner and neared our house. How many were there? It looked like fifteen, no, more followed—maybe thirty. In their midst was the Nazarene!

I recognized his voice as the rabbi speaking in the square last week. I had dared not look at him that day, but there was no shame in listening. So I had listened as I inched my way from market stall to market stall, pretending to inspect each fig and weigh the wheat over and over. I was an expert at listening. As a little girl, I listened from outside the synagogue as men read and sang the sacred texts. Spellbound and lost in their beauty, I drank them in and savored their sounds and meaning. As my brother tried to memorize his lessons perfectly, I silently copied the words in my head and stored them up for late night wrestling.

The Pentateuch, the Psalms, the Proverbs, the Prophets—sacred words weaving our history into the story of our glorious God. We are his portion, his people. The Nazarene's words sounded like sacred words from newer, different pages—but words of truth and beauty too. And now that voice was at my door.

My brother Lazarus was greeting them all, embracing and kissing and laughing, welcoming them into our home. They packed into every corner, sitting on chairs, lounging on the floor, nesting on windowsills. My brother's voice was eager and excited. He knew the Nazarene. He called him friend. I did not know his face but well I knew his words. Since that day in the square and late into the night, Lazarus and I debated his parables and stories. "Could he mean that?" "No, it was impossible." It sounded like he was contradicting the priests. Yet . . . they were words of justice and truth. Words echoing in my head . . .

"Bring everything from the storage bins," my sister barked. She was already in the kitchen, emptying vats of oil and baskets of wheat into large bowls to begin meal preparations. Focused and determined, she began the production to create a feast worthy of our guests. I hauled in everything I could find, one ear listening to her instructions and the other ear listening to conversations where the men had gathered in the front room. The buzz quieted. Now only one voice was heard—his voice.

"*A farmer went out to sow his seed . . .*"

"Mary, come and sift the wheat."

"*The teachers of the law and the Pharisees who sit in Moses' seat tell you this, but I say . . .*"

"Mary, I need you to knead the bread dough."

"*I tell you the truth, unless you change and become like a little child, you will never enter the kingdom of heaven . . .*"

"Mary, come and make a paste of the olives."

No, I won't stay in the kitchen. I must find out what it means to be a little child again. I'll stand by the doorway and listen, for just a little while. Then I'll go back and help. But I must hear him finish this part. What good are bits and pieces when nothing fits together? I must hear the whole story, just this once.

Hinged between the wall and the door, I listened as he finished the story . . . then there was silence. It sounded like he was rising, walking. Suddenly he was before me; I was discovered. Jesus peered around the door and our eyes met. I was embarrassed, humiliated, shamed. I had looked into his eyes! Had anyone seen? He didn't seem concerned. Smiling, warm, welcoming eyes beckoned.

Without a word, he called me to join them. He called me into the men's place of purpose, reason, reflection, conception, contemplation, and truth. I stepped out from my hiding place and followed him among silent gasps and questions. There next to his feet on the floor was an empty space that heaven had carved out just for me. I gathered my robes around me, secured my shawl, and curled up in that sweet little spot. He began to speak. I looked up and was reborn.

■   ■   ■

What you have just read is historical fiction. What actually transpired that day, resulting in Mary's decision to leave the kitchen to learn at the feet of Jesus? No one knows for sure. We do know that Jesus commended Mary for her decision—"Mary has chosen what is better, and it will not be taken away from her" (Luke 10:42). And

John reveals a tender relationship between them. "Jesus *loved* Martha and her sister and Lazarus" (John 11:5). Jesus was a guest in their home (John 12:1–2). When her brother was dying, Mary immediately sent for Jesus with the expectation that he would put down what he was doing and come to her aid. "So the sisters sent word to Jesus, 'Lord, the one you love is sick'" (John 11:3).[1] Just days before the crucifixion, Jesus commended Mary again for a bold act.

> Then Mary took about a pint of pure nard, an expensive perfume; she poured it on Jesus' feet and wiped his feet with her hair. . . .
> But one of his disciples, Judas Iscariot, who was later to betray him, objected. . . .
> "Leave her alone," Jesus replied. "It was intended that she should save this perfume for the day of my burial." (John 12:3–7)

His disciples struggled to understand and accept God's redemptive plan (Luke 18:31–34; 22:24–38; John 16:17–18), but Mary may have understood that Jesus came to die, and she expressed this insight by anointing his body for burial.[2] How did she learn except from the lips of Jesus himself? And why did she believe and consent when others close to him rejected the possibility of the cross? We observe hints of a deep friendship.

Jesus and Mary were friends in a culture where mixed-gender friendships were unusual. Like some places in the Middle East today, Jewish women in the first century were uneducated and undervalued. For example, they were not considered trustworthy enough to be witnesses in trials.[3] If a daughter made a vow, her father could annul it, as could a husband for his wife (Num. 30:2–16). Women were considered to be temptresses, as evidenced by a common practice among some religious leaders. These were labeled "bleeding" Pharisees because they walked with their eyes cast down in case a woman might come into view and tempt them.[4]

In this environment, Jesus extended the hand of friendship to Mary, and women have benefited from his boldness and inclusiveness ever since. The culture hindered it, but Jesus would not be bound by an unjust culture. It's very difficult for twenty-first-century Christians to fathom the courage required for Jesus to extend the hand of friendship to Mary in the first-century Jewish culture—and for Mary to step out and respond to his overture.

What was Jesus doing? He was destroying the centuries-old dividing wall that had kept women from full status as human beings created in the image of God. That wall is still standing in some places today, sometimes subtly, sometimes overtly. But for those who follow Christ, he cleared a different path—the path of friendship. As a loving big brother, he invited Mary into the dialogue in the living room.

Jesus applied Genesis 2:18, "It is not good for the man to be alone," to more than the marriage context. It is not good for men and women to isolate themselves from one another, such as the Taliban custom. *But women have not worn the veil in civilized progressive nations for a long time*, you might argue. That is true. But there has been a dividing wall nevertheless. It is a wall of the mind.

Fear of mixed-gender friendship is understandable in an oversexed society like ours. Women are not veiled; instead they are publicly undressed—also dehumanizing. It's no wonder Christian men and women put on blinders in an attempt to honor God with pure hearts and minds. But Jesus did not respond to women in fear. He knew that this wall of fear would exclude women from the public square of faith, and it has.

Please don't misunderstand. We are not saying that women should step in and take over the church or the home. We believe godly men should lead there. But in many churches, and even some Christian homes, women *are* kept in the back room—not physically but emotionally, spiritually, and intellectually. In many contexts, women are not privy to the discussions that count. They have been set off to the side, sometimes given permission to minister to one another, but often without resources or value. We don't believe this is malicious or even intentional. Often, men are simply protecting their integrity or their turf. Sometimes, it's simply because men and women don't know how to relate to one another as friends.

Jill works full-time ministering to women in the local church. Her e-mail to Sue expresses the echo we hear often behind closed doors.

Perhaps we should offer some breakout sessions on how to navigate the male world, how to get your male leadership to "want your voice" on the team. I am disturbed about this issue of women not being heard or supported. I think what I'm experiencing is "grieving." It breaks my heart to think about what is going on inside God's body. The world is so desperately in need of the church and for whatever reason we aren't willing to "unleash" every soldier. Why? Why do we do that? Why wouldn't we want *every* individual unleashed, equipped, and supported to our fullest ability on God's behalf? I just don't understand. My heart really is breaking.

I met with Doris who ministered at her church on the side, unpaid, because she loves Jesus and wants to serve his people. Finally she gets hired because she does such a good job, yet they keep her on the outside. They want to make sure she "stays in her place." I have watched and seen her heart change. It's become a battle from within the leadership, it takes all she has to navigate the inside, and it's sucked the passion right out of her. I have watched her soul go from being a flame to being a flicker. God cannot be pleased about this. And she isn't the only one. I heard similar stories at the Association of Women's Ministry Professionals meeting last month.

Sue, why aren't there more men like my pastor, championing the way? Don't we want to be a "church" that is all about fighting for Jesus? Isn't there enough work to be done that we need *all* of us? Hear me, I'm not mad at men. I think most of them don't have a clue they are doing it. And I know most have good hearts, but where is this blindness coming from? I also know that change will only come if initiated by men, because otherwise the men think it's a power play by the women. Why can't we get there?[5]

Men and women are different, but sometimes we overemphasize the differences and discount the similarities. There is this light-hearted attitude that men and women can't understand one another. After all, they are from different planets.[6] How could they possibly work together? In reality, that is part of the sex game. We say women are mysterious and that makes them enticing. Women play into the role without thinking. It is all part of the fun. But the by-product of the game is that often women are excluded from the discussion. Jesus would not play the game, and neither should we.

As we will see in the following pages, Jesus reached out to women in the first century. He knew it was not good for men to live in isolation from half of the human race. Men are alone when they refuse the companionship and camaraderie of women. They are alone when they discount female ideas and input. They are alone when they deny the good that might result from women's creativity and giftedness. Carolyn Custis James puts it well:

> The war zone is no respecter of gender. The inclusion of women in the ranks of God's army is not to meet some affirmative action requirement or to ensure women receive the same treatment as the men. The simple yet revolutionary reason for including women is because the army needs them.
>
> God never intended for women to sit on the sidelines and await the outcome of the battle the men are fighting. He meant for us to be theologically active and engaged right alongside the men on the front lines of the battle. Our fellow soldiers bear a double burden if women march unarmed into battle. And they are doubly protected if we prepare ourselves for combat.

In a battle fierce as this, brave warriors are indispensable
whether they are male or female.[7]

Throughout his earthly ministry, Jesus extended the hand of
friendship to women. Let's look at other examples of the way Jesus
befriended women, with an eye to following in his steps.

Guess Who's Coming to Dinner

What did the Twelve think about Jesus befriending women?
Before he was crucified, they struggled with many of his ideas and
teachings (Luke 18:31–34). They jockeyed to sit at his right hand
(Luke 22:24–30). Peter insisted he would never betray him regardless of the cost (Luke 22:33). They argued with Jesus when he told
them he was going to the cross. Imagine how they reacted when he
treated women as sisters. Were they perplexed when he disregarded
the cultural mores that devalued women? We are not told explicitly
although we can read between the lines in several gospel accounts
where Jesus stands up for women. Let's look again at the account,
this time from Mark's gospel, when Mary anoints Jesus for burial.
The story begins at a dinner party in Jesus' honor just a few days
before the crucifixion.

> While he was in Bethany, reclining at the table in the home
> of a man known as Simon the Leper, a woman came with an
> alabaster jar of very expensive perfume, made of pure nard.
> She broke the jar and poured the perfume on his head.
>   Some of those present were saying indignantly to one an-
> other, "Why this waste of perfume? It could have been sold
> for more than a year's wages and the money given to the
> poor." And they rebuked her harshly.
>   "Leave her alone," said Jesus. "Why are you bothering
> her? She has done a beautiful thing to me. The poor you
> will always have with you, and you can help them any time
> you want. But you will not always have me. She did what she
> could. She poured perfume on my body beforehand to pre-

pare for my burial. I tell you the truth, wherever the gospel is preached throughout the world, what she has done will also be told, in memory of her." (Mark 14:3–9)

Here we see Mary again, the same woman who sat at Jesus' feet.[8] Mary was accused by the other dinner guests of being wasteful.

Another dinner party and similarly misunderstood extravagance takes place in the classic story *Babette's Feast*. Babette, a French woman, is hired to serve as a cook in a bleak and rigidly religious parish whose residents wear black and eat gruel made from boiled bread and cod. After twelve years of thankless service to the grim villagers, Babette won ten thousand francs in the French lottery.

Shortly thereafter, she orders the necessary ingredients to prepare a meal, a real French meal. For weeks the villagers watch as extravagance after extravagance appears in town: cases of champagne, huge tortoises, truffles, pheasants, and fresh vegetables, all delivered to Babette's kitchen. The community frowns upon the coming "witch's brew." They agree to eat the French meal, but will withhold their comments—tongues were meant for praise and thanksgiving, not for indulging in exotic tastes.

Babette pours out her culinary talent, and her unparalleled feast is a success. In the concluding conversation, a woman commends Babette's feast and assumes that she will soon return to Paris, but Babette says that she cannot afford the trip. The woman asks, "But what about the ten thousand francs?" Babette explains that she has spent every last franc on the feast the villagers had vowed not to enjoy, but had devoured nonetheless.

In his book *What's So Amazing About Grace?* author Philip Yancey says of the story, "Grace came to them in the form of a feast . . . a meal of a lifetime lavished on those who had in no way earned it, who barely possessed the faculties to receive it."[9]

Much like the guests at Babette's dinner party, the disciples who watched as Mary anointed Jesus piously accused her of foolishness and impracticality. They could not understand the meaning of her extravagant sacrifice.

Jesus came to Mary's defense magnificently. We can see him standing to his feet as he rebuked them. *Leave her alone. Stop bothering her.* Can you hear the emotion in his voice? He was like an offended big brother coming to the rescue of his little sister. Then he explained that her actions were not silly; in fact, they were insightful and prophetic. Of all the people in the room, she alone may have understood that he was going to die soon, and although she grieved, she expressed her concession and trust. Did she understand its significance? Was she spiritually attuned to the realities of why he came and what he was going to do? We can't be sure. But Jesus praised her for her actions and weighed them as pure and good. Then he declared that she would have a place in his spiritual hall of fame forever. What a humbling experience for the others in the room! Their pride and ego took a beating that day when Jesus let everyone know it was dangerous to mess with his sister.

> I am convinced that partnering with women will significantly enhance ministry. In a male-dominated ministry culture, men see things from a male perspective. A female perspective will enhance every aspect of ministry—from children's work and youth work, to the kind of sermons preached on Sunday and the quality of seminary education. We must remember that women are half (probably more than half) of the Christian population. If ministry is to be successful, it needs leaders who understand all of those to whom they minister—male and female.
>
> —Dr. Frank James

How did the Twelve treat women after watching Jesus for over three years? Did they mimic Jesus' sibling love or acquiesce to the culture? How did they interact with women after the resurrection and ascension and in their future ministries? The issues were as complex for them as they are for us today. Ministering in cultures that devalue and mistreat women affects us all. But Jesus' example in Mark 14 stands out as a stark contrast to his culture and should empower us all to stand in the face of any culture that attempts to devalue or degrade women.

Walking Partners

My (Sue's) Bible study had been learning about leadership, using the apostles in the New Testament as our primary examples. Over and over the teacher applied his lesson to the men in the group, even though the group was more than 60 percent women. We women simply did the mental gymnastics to turn his words into sound lessons for women, too, and did so without resentment. We loved our teacher and knew the exclusion was not malicious.

But several weeks into the series, a woman in the back asked this question:

> *Do you think that others walked with Jesus and learned from him besides the twelve apostles?*

Hidden in her question, she was asking, "Did Jesus call women into significant service too?" The teacher and several other men in the room responded, again applying the text to men only. Finally, I read Luke 8:1–3 aloud:

> After this, Jesus traveled about from one town and village to another, proclaiming the good news of the kingdom of God. The Twelve were with him, and also some women who had been cured of evil spirits and diseases: Mary (called Magdalene) from whom seven demons had come out; Joanna the wife of Cuza, the manager of Herod's household; Susanna; and many others. These women were helping to support them out of their own means.

The teacher welcomed my words and thanked me for my insight. The woman who asked the question mouthed "*thank you*" from across the room, and several other women thanked me afterward. I did not read Luke 8:1–3 with an edge, nor did the woman who asked the

question have an agenda. The women in the room were not angry
with their teacher. They did not believe this fine Christian man
intentionally excluded them. They did not leave murmuring under
their breath that this man was insensitive or chauvinistic. They
gave their brother the benefit of the doubt. They would even have
defended their brother, insisting that he was oblivious to the way
he had presented the lesson. But even for these women, there came
a time when they wanted to be included. They wanted to know if
Jesus cared for them and had a plan and place for them too.

> The world as it has evolved has become more and more
> intolerant of environments that don't bring in a woman's
> voice. For example, my daughters—ages twenty-one and
> twenty-six—would never enter a world where a woman's
> voice was not represented in the church. I see a growing
> presence of women in the postmodern world, and the en-
> vironments that do not include women will die.
>
> —Dr. Dan Allender

This scenario is played out in pulpits and in Sunday school and
seminary classrooms throughout the country every day. Women are
unintentionally excluded in the rhetoric or the application by well-
meaning men. Most Christian women give their brothers the benefit
of the doubt over and over, vowing not to develop a grudge or carry
a chip on their shoulders. But deep in their hearts, they yearn to
hear that Jesus cared for women too. Did Jesus intentionally include
women? According to the verses citing women as walking partners
(Luke 8:1–3), he did.

No, Jesus did not choose a woman as one of the twelve apostles.
He prayed fervently over whom God wanted, and no women were
called (Luke 6:12–16). But that does not mean that Jesus did not
befriend or include women on his journey throughout Israel and
ultimately to the cross. Luke makes a point of telling us that some
women came along—in fact *many* women came along. We know the
names of three and we know that these women were wealthy, and

Jesus accepted their money to supply the needs of their group as they traveled.

How do you picture their wanderings? Do you see Jesus and the twelve apostles walking along immersed in deep, important conversations while the little band of obscure women followed far behind bringing up the rear in silence, weighted down with gold to be doled out as needs arose? Do you really think that Jesus would have allowed this oriental custom in his entourage? Would the man who welcomed Mary to sit at his feet have ignored and excluded other passionate women like Mary Magdalene, Joanna, and Susanna from learning and engaging as they sojourned together? No. Jesus intentionally included them in a culture where women were undervalued.

> If women don't have opportunity in the church, they often express their gifts in the marketplace. I have seen it happen for thirty years. And I think it's a terrible thing. Many male church leaders and male elders will stand accountable before God someday for that. To me it's a blind spot in the minds and the hearts of church leaders in many places around the world. If I were the Evil One and could figure out a way to deny the local church, the hope of the world, about 50 percent of its horsepower—I would work very hard to do that in one fell swoop. If I could relegate one half of the church to the sidelines, strategically it's a pretty smart move.
>
> —Bill Hybels[10]

One Powerful Little Word

While Jesus was still talking to the crowd, his mother and brothers stood outside, wanting to speak to him. Someone told him, "Your mother and brothers are standing outside, wanting to speak to you."

He replied to him, "Who is my mother, and who are my brothers?" Pointing to his disciples, he said, "Here are my mother and my brothers. For whoever does the will of my Father in heaven is my brother and sister and mother." (Matt. 12:46–50)

In chapter 1, we saw Jesus teaching the world that he came to create a whole new kind of family—a faith family. He told his biological family that this new family took precedent. But there is another lesson hidden in his response that shows his special concern for women. Look back at the passage. What is the word Jesus adds when he points to his disciples? Can you find it?

Who does Jesus include in the list of family members that was not mentioned before? Sisters! Women are included in Jesus' family! This might seem like a small thing to some, but to the marginalized women in the first century, this was tantamount to words of life. And they are still words of life to women today.

The Lord made a point to remind everyone that sisters are part of the forever family too. Jesus, the Master Communicator, added one simple word that made a great difference to half the human race. If Jesus could make the mental effort to add that one simple word of inclusion, why can't preachers and teachers and husbands and fathers do the same today? Little words are powerful, and Jesus took the time to add them so as to express the truth—that we are all brothers and sisters, called to walk alongside the Savior together. If men of influence take this to heart and include women in their rhetoric, what a difference it would make!

In this chapter we have laid out three examples of Jesus befriending women in the face of the first-century culture. He was probably criticized for it, but he didn't care. Some things are too important to let culture dictate, and for Jesus this was one of them. Over the years, I (Sue) have counseled many frustrated and wounded women who ask, "Why is it so difficult to work with men?"

Why do some men and women today struggle to take the stand that Jesus took? Why is it so difficult to see one another as siblings and to partner together as one family? There are many reasons. It is a complicated issue, especially in an oversexed society like ours. Walk with us as we wrestle with these issues, dialogue with experts, and seek God's answers. Jesus cared enough to make a place for Mary at his feet, to defend her when she was under attack, to include women in his parade, and to speak a little word that made a big difference. Let's follow in his footsteps.

DISCUSSION QUESTIONS

1. Jesus intentionally reached out to women in the first century. Do you see a similar heart attitude with most Christian men today? If so, what do you think motivates them? If not, what do you think hinders them?
2. Has someone of the opposite sex ever defended you? If so, describe what happened and how you felt.
3. Have you observed instances when preachers or teachers have offended the other gender? (No names, please.) If so, describe the situation. Do you think the offense was intentional?
4. Have you ever been slighted or offended by a preacher or teacher related to your gender? (No names, please.) Describe what happened and your response.
5. What can men and women do to better value and honor one another through their words and actions? Be specific.

Chapter 3

Paul—a Brother?

Dear God, maybe Cain and Abel would not kill each other so much if
they had their own rooms. It works with my brother.

—LARRY

A Tale of Two Brothers

A four-foot-tall spray of flowers—vivid yellows, rich purples, brilliant reds—stood between Megan and her front door. She was returning home from one of those special days—a day to remember. The church had joined in celebrating the publication of her first book. They announced the title from the pulpit, called her to the front, and prayed that her labor of love would impact people everywhere. They even set up a signing table and gave the congregation an opportunity to greet her and take home a copy. It was one of those blurry days—the kind of day that seems better than a real day.

Her husband sent her flowers on occasion, but not four feet of them. Something told her this giant bouquet was not from him—maybe because he was standing beside her gawking at the arrangement too. Tucked away among the blooms, she saw a card that read, *We are so proud of you—your church family.* So, these were from Gary, her boss. Now before you get any ideas, Gary often sent flowers to women on his staff.

After the service, Gary had treated Megan, her husband, and the entire staff to a delicious Italian lunch in honor of the author in their midst—and now this floral homecoming! Megan hauled them into the house and sat staring at them in blissful exhaustion, the way one does after a day to remember.

She sank back into an easy chair, feet propped up, enjoying an ice-cold bottle of water and thinking back to a different day—a day to forget. Ten years earlier she ministered in a different church where she also led the ministry to women. But that boss, senior pastor John, did not send her flowers. She could hardly have called him her boss because she was not on staff, although he supplied her with an ample budget. She clocked as many work hours as a full-time staffer, but her value was clarified one afternoon when he declared in her presence, "I will never have a woman on my staff."

In John's defense, he was a man of integrity—a fine preacher and evangelist. He led a prominent church on the front lines for God.

Megan rarely saw him. Shortly after accepting the position, she had the crazy idea that she should share her vision with the pastor. So she made an appointment. After passing through two secretaries, she entered into the inner sanctum. He was busy shuffling papers and did not look up for several minutes. Finally, he grunted at her to sit down. She reintroduced herself, thinking maybe he did not know who she was, but he did. He asked why she had come. Megan dribbled out a few words about how glad she was to be called to serve and her plan for the women's ministry. He looked back to his papers, and after a couple of icy minutes, she excused herself. Later she learned one never makes an appointment with John. He makes an appointment with you.

When you think of the apostle Paul's attitude toward women, do you think of Gary or do you think of John? For years we authors envisioned Paul with a "John" face—furrowed brow, glaring at women over his busy calendar, wondering why they were bothering him. Of late we see him more like Gary, with an open door and "yes" face. Why? We studied Paul's friendships with women. Was Paul a brother? What do we see if we examine his working relationships with women?

For fifty-five years I have been a promoter of women. It's a conviction of mine. The first occasion when I was really impressed with the power of women was when I was pastoring a church as a young man in Wichita, Kansas, and in that church was a wealthy couple—the Witts. Mrs. Witt was an outstanding Bible teacher. That woman was my cheerleader—she was on my team! She taught me so much and she also supported me. We became the closest of friends and remained so for many years until she went home to be with the Savior.

Other influential women in my life were Mary and Lois LeBar, instrumental Christian educators and authors. First we were classmates and later, when I studied at Wheaton, they were my teachers. Lois served as professor and chairperson of the Christian education department at Wheaton for many years. We were just like brother and sisters, and that was a great experience.

When I started a church in Ft. Worth—now McKinney Memorial Bible Church—I was deeply involved in establishing the women's ministry and working with women in a variety of settings.

Another great privilege was getting to know and work with Henrietta Mears at Hollywood's First Presbyterian Church. She asked me to speak and this was a tremendous opportunity. At the end of the week she invited me to her home and introduced me to a couple she suggested we keep our eye on—Bill and Vonette Bright, the future founders of Campus Crusade for Christ. I met them in her kitchen. Miss Mears was a remarkable woman, especially in her generation.

I also learned to respect women in my home growing up. I came from a broken home but my father was incredibly supportive of women. Once when I sassed my grandmother, he made it clear that this was unacceptable behavior. Men don't talk to women that way!

> I'm very comfortable ministering with women. I've grown up around them and I've developed great respect and honor for them.
>
> —Dr. Howard Hendricks

An Overview of Women in the New Testament

The Bible often presents its characters warts and all. They are painted as real people who mess up. Some recover; some don't. But, as we will see, in the New Testament, most women are presented in a positive light. A few women were temptresses, but when they met Jesus, they left that lifestyle.[1] We will look at their stories in a later chapter. Herodias and Salome, who conspired to have John the Baptist beheaded, are the exception, but these were not women of faith (Matt. 14:1–12). Overall, women in the New Testament, both Jew and Gentile, are portrayed as good models and godly sisters. New Testament authors gave women a place at the ministry table.

Why were women presented this way? Was it because male disciples understood that partnering with gifted women would strengthen their efforts to evangelize a needy world and build the infant church? Was it because so many women responded in faith? That seems to be a pattern throughout the centuries and continues today.[2] We can't say why women fare well on the pages of the New Testament—but, as we will show you, they do.

Some secular religious scholars today have a difficult time accepting this positive view of women in the New Testament. Some, such as Princeton religion professor Elaine Pagels, argue on the basis of weak and nonexistent evidence that Jesus did not relate to Mary Magdalene as a sister, but instead that theirs was a sexual relationship.[3] Dan Brown, who wrote *The DaVinci Code*, and filmmaker Sony, who produced the movie, capitalized on this notion.[4] They played to the hidden belief of many in our oversexed culture that a genuine platonic relationship between men and women is impossible—but the New Testament argues otherwise. Most women in its pages are presented as eager to follow Jesus, to serve in the church, and to partner with their brothers. Let's look more closely at specific examples.

Sisters in Rome

Sister Phoebe

It is impossible to measure the impact of the book of Romans on the Christian church. Possibly no other biblical literature has yielded more theological fruit than this important letter. It is remarkable that in a culture where a woman's word was not trusted as testimony in a trial,[5] Paul's emissary to deliver this letter was a woman.[6] He trusted her not to lose the letter. He trusted her to find her way to Rome. He trusted her to get the letter into the right hands. He ended the letter with these words:

> I commend to you our sister Phoebe, a servant of the church in Cenchrea. I ask you to receive her in the Lord in a way worthy of the saints and to give her any help she may need from you, for she has been a great help to many people, including me. (Rom. 16:1–2)

We don't know much about Phoebe except that Paul used the word *diakonon* to describe her. *Diakonon* is often translated as "minister" in other New Testament passages.[7] This is the same word used for the office of deacon in Philippians 1:1 and 1 Timothy 3:8, 10, 12. John Witmer comments that "use of the word with the phrase 'of the church' strongly suggests some recognized position, a fact appropriate for a person serving as Paul's emissary."[8] We can't be absolutely sure she held a recognized office but she must have been a woman of tremendous integrity and influence. Imagine the time and effort it took for Paul to write the letter to the Romans. He would only entrust it to a reliable messenger.

We see Paul commending her as a hardworking woman worthy of honor and asking the church in Rome to give her whatever she needs. She has been a "great help to many people, including me," writes Paul (Rom. 16:2). What kind of a woman would be a great help to an "Energizer bunny" like Paul? We can only imagine her abilities, her resourcefulness, and her stamina. Paul was not one to put up with sissies. Look at his refusal to take unreliable John Mark with him on his second journey (Acts 15:36–40).

He also used the word *prostates* to describe her. Some translate this word as "helper," but a more accurate translation is "protectress."[9] This is not a word describing someone cleaning toilets or baking cookies, although both tasks are honorable when done to serve the Lord and others. This is a word fitting a strong, trusted leader in the church, a reliable coworker. Who or what did she protect? We don't know, although obviously she protected Paul's manuscript.

> I look at a passage like Romans 16 where Paul lists all the people who made an impact in his ministry, and what overwhelms me is the large number of women, and his comments about them.
>
> —Dr. Howard Hendricks

How it must have encouraged Phoebe when the Roman congregation read this letter. How kind of Paul to open the door for her there. It might have taken her years to gain the trust of the Romans, but with just a few words from the apostle Paul, she was in. It must have warmed her heart to hear these words praising her abilities and trustworthiness, but there was another word in the accolades that may have been even more precious.

It is one thing to serve alongside someone and be appreciated for your abilities and hard work. It is another to be included in their family. Paul called Phoebe his sister. It is a term of endearment. It means that she is worth more than what she can do. She is not valuable to him just because she is efficient; she is honored and loved for who she is. She is his sister!

Sister Priscilla

Have you ever read a book insisting that women are relational but men are not? We the authors have, but we think that Paul dispels this error in Romans 16. Male and female friendships may look different but both are called to meaningful, personal relationships.

Romans 16 reveals that Paul had many male and female friends and
that he knew their whereabouts. He kept up with his friends. Paul
was a people-person, as evidenced by his long list of personal saluta-
tions. He mentions twenty-six by name and refers to many others.
At least ten are women. In the Roman culture, where women were
regarded as property and second-class citizens, this is astonishing.[10]

The first person he greets in Rome was female—Priscilla, along
with her husband, Aquila (Rom. 16:3). He commended this couple
for their courage. They put their life on the line for Paul. What exactly did they do? Again, we don't know, but whatever it was, Paul
was extremely grateful.

It is interesting to note that, contrary to custom, Priscilla's name
is listed first. In an earlier letter, Paul greeted the couple as "Aquila
and Priscilla" (1 Cor. 16:19), but all other mentions of the couple list
her first (Acts 18:18–19, 26; 2 Tim. 4:19). We might conclude that
of the two, she may have been the more public figure. We have precedent for this conclusion. When Paul and Barnabas begin to minister as a team, Barnabas's name is listed first, but over time as Paul
became the more prominent, we observe the order of their names
reversed (Acts 12:25; 13:2; reversal after Acts 13:42).

Paul met Priscilla and Aquila on his second missionary journey
when their paths crossed in Corinth. We don't know if Priscilla and
Aquila were Christians before they met Paul, but the Bible paints
them as coworkers and friends.[11] They shared the same occupation—
tent making—and they lived and worked together for several years
(Acts 18:1–3, 11, 18). Imagine the friendship that blossomed over
"talking shop." Paul never missed an opportunity to train eager students, and Priscilla and Aquila must have been perceptive pupils.

When Paul left Corinth to plant a church in Ephesus, the couple left with him. And when Paul left Ephesus, Priscilla and Aquila
stayed behind to nurture the newborn church (Acts 18:18–21). Priscilla was an accomplished theologian and teacher, as evidenced by
her active role in Apollos's instruction in their home (Acts 18:24–
28). Her prominence does not diminish her husband's honor. He
may have been endowed with gifts that made him more effective in

the background. This does not make him less in the eyes of God nor does it make her more so, although some people tend to judge that way.

Priscilla's public prominence makes some Christians uncomfortable. In their mind, the male must lead and the female must follow. But often, God does not gift couples this way. Sometimes it is the woman who has the upfront gifts and the husband who is gifted in administration, mercy, or serving. Elisabeth Elliot, who gained worldwide attention when her first husband, missionary Jim Elliot, was killed by the Aucas in Ecuador, became a widely sought-after speaker in Christian circles. Her husband, Lars Gren, served as her manager. She was the face and voice of their ministry, yet his contributions were vital to its success. It is the world that values the upfront gifts more—not God. He honors both those who work in the limelight and those who work behind the stage. God weighs with different weights.

As we examine Paul's relationship with Priscilla and Phoebe, we see a brother and his sisters standing strong as witnesses for Jesus together. And we see platonic, nonsexual friendships. We see them acting like sacred siblings.

Other Roman Relatives

Paul used the language of family as he continued greeting others so dear to him in Rome. Look at all the women included.

> Greet Mary, who worked very hard for you.
> Greet Andronicus and Junias, my relatives
>   who have been in prison with me. They are
>   outstanding among the apostles, and they were
>   in Christ before I was. . . .
> Greet Tryphena and Tryphosa, those women who
>   work hard in the Lord.
> Greet my dear friend Persis, another woman who
>   has worked very hard in the Lord.

> Greet Rufus, chosen in the Lord, and his mother,
> who has been a mother to me, too. . . .
> Greet . . . Julia, Nereus and his sister, and Olympas
> and all the saints with them.
>
> (Rom. 16:6–15)

Like women today, sisters worked hard in the early church.[12] That refrain is echoed over and over in these verses. Some were commended for their courage, suffering in prison alongside their brothers. And some were leaders, as seen in Phoebe, Priscilla, and possibly Junia.[13] The tone and sense of the passage is clear and beautiful—these women served alongside Paul as brother and sisters—modeling for us today!

Sisters in Philippi

On one of his missionary journeys, Paul changed his travel plans midstream, setting his sail for the continent of Europe after seeing a vision of a man from Macedonia calling for help (Acts 16:6–10). But the first to respond to the good news of Jesus in Europe was not a man but a woman. Her name was Lydia. Paul found her gathered with other women down by the river outside the city gates (Acts 16:13). Luke describes Lydia as a "worshiper of God" or a God-seeker (Acts 16:14). She was a Gentile who heard about the one true God and wanted to know him—and he wanted her to know him. So he sent Paul to Philippi. She was probably a widow because the passage talks about "her household,"[14] and wives in that time were not property owners.[15] We also learn from the text that she was an astute businesswoman, a dealer in fine fabrics, and that she housed Paul and his friends during their stay in Philippi. She was also hostess to the first church in Europe, which met in her home (Acts 16:6–15).

It is likely that the other women who heard Paul's message down by the river came to faith, as did many others in Philippi during Paul's ministry there. Like Jesus, Paul did not run from the river when he saw a company of women there. He sat down and talked with them. He saw their need for Jesus and he reached out to them as he would to a sister. He saw them as persons first—not as sexual beings, not as temptresses out to snare him. He built the church in Philippi on the faith of these earnest women who wanted to know Jesus. And the church there thrived.[16]

Ten years after their meeting by the river, Paul wrote a letter to his beloved Philippians and he began with a beautiful prayer. Imagine what Lydia and the other women thought as they read Paul's prayer for the first time.

> I thank my God every time I remember you. In all my prayers for all of you, I always pray with joy because of your partnership in the gospel from the first day until now, being confident of this, that he who began a good work in you will carry it on to completion until the day of Christ Jesus.
>
> It is right for me to feel this way about all of you, since I have you in my heart; for whether I am in chains or defending and confirming the gospel, all of you share in God's grace with me. God can testify how I long for all of you with the affection of Christ Jesus.
>
> And this is my prayer: that your love may abound more and more in knowledge and depth of insight, so that you may be able to discern what is best and may be pure and blameless until the day of Christ, filled with the fruit of righteousness that comes through Jesus Christ—to the glory and praise of God. (Phil. 1:3–11)

Now there is a sibling's prayer. Paul prays that these women, and all the believers there, might live pure lives, filled with righteousness. He shares how he loves them with a holy love and how he desires God's best for each one, regardless of gender. Their sweet sibling relationship is expressed in every line. It is not wrong for brothers and sisters to love one another with this holy kind of Christian love. What a wonderful partnership for all of us to emulate as brothers and sisters in Christ!

Sisters in Crete

Paul made sure that his sisters in the early church received quality mentoring and sound teaching. How do we know? By studying his letter to Titus, a minister on the island of Crete. Crete is a beautiful Greek island in the Aegean Sea where Paul planted churches. He took Titus with him and apparently many responded to the gospel because he left Titus behind to "straighten out what was left unfinished and appoint elders in every town, as I directed you" (Titus 1:5).

Crete was not an easy place to work—even today it is an insult to call someone a Cretan. Paul described them as "rebellious people, mere talkers and deceivers" (Titus 1:10). He quoted the Cretan poet Epimenides who wrote, "Cretans are always liars, evil brutes, lazy gluttons" (Titus 1:12). Paul warned Titus that Crete would not be an easy place to grow strong, healthy churches. Along with specific instructions for men, Paul's blueprint for strong, healthy churches included vibrant ministries to women.

> You must teach what is in accord with sound doctrine. Teach the older men to be temperate, worthy of respect, self-controlled, and sound in faith, in love and in endurance.
>
> Likewise, teach the older women to be reverent in the way they live, not to be slanderers or addicted to much wine, but to teach what is good. Then they can train the younger women to love their husbands and children, to be self-controlled and pure, to be busy at home, to be kind, and to be subject to their husbands, so that no one will malign the word of God.
>
> Similarly, encourage the young men to be self-controlled. In everything set them an example by doing what is good. (Titus 2:1–7)

Titus was instructed to teach sound doctrine and character development to the older men, the younger men, and the older women, but *not* the younger women. Interestingly, Paul specifically instructed Titus to delegate the care and instruction of the younger women to the older women. We might misconstrue this to mean that Paul wanted to segregate the men from the women. But we know that is not true, because Paul enjoyed personal friendships with many women, as we have just observed.

Why then this advice? We believe that Paul understood that older women make better teachers, trainers, mentors, and models for younger women because, as women, they have so much in common. And Paul wanted his sisters to get the best possible care and instruction.

Let's examine the text carefully. Paul instructs Titus to teach the older women. The term *older* does not necessarily refer to chronological age. It means "advanced in the process,"[17] and the term *younger* women means "early in the process."[18] Some younger women exhibit spiritual maturity that qualifies them to minister in the church. However, it is true that the longer we live, the more experience we gain to pass on to others. There are advantages to age, but young people are not disqualified from ministering.

Paul is instructing Titus to identify mature women and get them ready to be put in charge of the other women in the church. Paul's instructions were countercultural. Remember that women had little opportunity for formal education and no theological training.[19] Paul was more concerned with the care and instruction of his sisters than with social mores. Titus's role was to prime the pump and then hand over the ministry to the mature women.

How could Titus tell who was mature and who was not? Paul pointed out core qualities to look for in his attempt to identify women leaders. These same qualifications apply today. First, Titus should look for a woman who was reverent in the way she lived (Titus 2:3). What does that mean? This kind of woman loves God with a holy reverence and she lives out of that relationship. She is genuine. She is the same women in private that she is in public. If you followed her around for a day, you would see that she walks her talk. If you are a woman who wants to serve the Lord, this is the kind of woman you must strive to become. If you are a man looking for a sister to work with you, this is the kind of woman to look for.

Next Paul talked about two negative qualities that disqualify a woman from leading. She must not be a slanderer and she must not be addicted to much wine (Titus 2:3). Slanderers are women who do not control their tongues. How destructive is a loose tongue? If you want to care for and instruct others, you must learn to speak graciously, with respect and kindness, at the right time, and with wisdom. Leaders are privy to information that can ruin lives if it is shared carelessly. Leaders must use words to build up and not tear down. A loose tongue disqualifies sisters from leadership and, in our experience, brothers and sisters alike are leery of working with women who talk foolishly or excessively.

We have also observed that slander, gossip, and foolish words often lead to conflict in ministry. And too often this conflict is sourced in women. Why is it that Solomon writes about contentious *women* who drive their husbands to rooftops to escape (Prov. 21:9)? We have also observed that if women are not cared for and valued in the church, they tend to be contentious. They may appear to be calm on the outside but they are fuming on the inside—the result is conflict and strife. But when women are respected and treated like sisters, they tend toward less conflict and gossip, even when they don't agree. The lesson is for brothers to value their sisters and give them a voice at the table. Make sure women receive quality shepherding from equipped sisters. And sisters, make sure you control your tongues!

The other disqualifier Paul mentions is alcoholism—but we believe this can be applied to any addiction. Drunkenness was a problem on Crete, but there are multiple addictions and distractions that keep women from loving and serving God effectively. Paul wanted the sisters in Crete to be taught by women free from addiction and, instead, sold out to Jesus!

Today women lose themselves in careers, exercise, body image, materialism, and even family. All these endeavors are fine in moderation but overdosing harms a sister's emotional, mental, and spiritual health—and brother Paul cared about all three.

After Titus identified and trained these mature women, what were they to do? They were to teach what is good (Titus 2:3). The word for *teach* here is the same word used for male teachers and preachers. It is used of rabbis and doctors. It is formal, in-depth teaching.[20] We believe Paul builds a case for women teaching women Bible and theology. Too many women's ministries are centered around fluffy events instead of ministries that transform lives. Paul tells Titus to make sure the sisters receive formal Scripture teaching from trained women—and the mandate holds today. Men, if you want women to be mature and godly, you must provide them with women who can teach them God's Word.

Mature women are then instructed to "train the younger women" (Titus 2:4). The word translated *train* here is different from formal teaching. It is sourced in the word *wisdom,* which means "skill in living."[21] There may only be a handful of women qualified to teach God's Word in a church, but the church needs an army of prepared women competent to train the younger women. These are the mentors, spiritual mothers, coaches, and counselors who come alongside less mature women and show them how to live as godly sisters.

Paul lists some of the character qualities that women need to develop (Titus 2:4–5). On Crete most women were probably wives and mothers who worked alongside their husbands. Today, however, 45 percent of women are single.[22] Sixty percent of women work outside the home.[23] How does a single woman exhibit purity at work? How does a working mother decide between conflicting job and family demands? Today's women need additional skills and wisdom to navigate our complex world. Women leaders minister to a diverse population of women who expect excellence and expertise. Caring brothers, like Paul, provide equipped, trained women for their beloved sisters.

Brothers to Emulate

The New Testament pictures Paul working alongside women as a brother, as illustrated by his friendships with women in Rome and Philippi, and by his instructions for their teaching and training in Crete. Like Jesus, he stood in the face of a culture that discounted women as peripheral.[24] Paul, like Jesus, had the best interests of his sisters at heart. Neither was afraid to develop a woman's gifts and give her a significant place to serve.

Jesus and Paul are exemplary models for Christian men everywhere and for all time. They were brothers to Christian women! This is a message seldom proclaimed but we believe it is time for a change. If we really want to be Christlike or follow in the steps of the apostle Paul, we must adopt a new family paradigm—we must see and treat one another as siblings. We believe this new mind-set would revolutionize ministry today, put to rest the heated debate over women's role in the church, and bring honor to God as the culture observes us acting like family.

DISCUSSION QUESTIONS

1. In the past, have you considered Paul a brother to women? Why or why not?
2. Paul's letters contain sections that seem to limit and devalue women (1 Cor. 11:1–16; 14:34–36; 1 Tim. 2:11–15). How do you reconcile these passages with Paul's friendships with women presented in the chapter?
3. Paul lists Priscilla's name first when he refers to the couple. Does this make you uncomfortable? What is your response when a wife has more upfront gifts and a husband serves in the background?
4. In your opinion, what kinds of leadership roles are appropriate for women today?
5. Read 1 Corinthians 13:4–7, inserting the words *a sister* or *a brother* according to your gender in place of the word *love*. (For example, "*a sister* is patient . . ." or "*a brother* is kind . . .") Or if you are discussing the questions with a group, read the verses aloud, rotating the words *a sister* and *a brother* each time love is mentioned. As you apply these verses, what are the implications for the way you treat the opposite sex, especially those on staff with whom you work?

Chapter 4

It's a Family Thing

*The highlight of my childhood was making my brother laugh so hard
that food came out his nose.*
—GARRISON KEILLOR

*Siblings are the people we practice on, the people who teach us about fair-
ness and cooperation and kindness and caring—quite often the hard way.*
—PAMELA DUGDALE

Sexual Norms

Brothers and Sisters Within the Biological Family

Think back to your childhood. Your older brother gets old enough
to think girls are pretty cool, not to mention just pretty. After a couple of years, the girls start thinking he's kind of cute too. His dating
life takes off, and before you know it, he's got a steady girlfriend.

Eeuww, gross! you, the preadolescent younger sister, think. *What does
she see in him? How can she stand to even kiss him? Ick!*

Fast-forward a few years, to young adulthood. You've matured
enough to become actual friends with your brother. You can admit that he is an attractive, good-looking guy who deserves his fair
share of female attention. But no matter how close your relationship,

no matter what he looks like, you are not the least bit physically attracted to him yourself.

Is your brother a man? Of course. Does he have all the correct body parts, hormones, and genetics that other males have? Yes. So why is he different from any other guy you might become attracted to? Why isn't he sexually appealing to you?

Because he's not a "real" guy—he's your *brother!* He's that other child of your parents, who even looks a little like you, who shares your family and history and heritage. Your love for him does not involve one bit of sexual attraction.

Sarah Sumner, in her book *Men and Women in the Church*, reflects on the time she shared an apartment with her brother when they were both in their twenties. "For him, it was taboo to think of me, his sister, as a potential sexual partner. I was 'just Sarah' to him. He thought of me as 'Sis.' So far was he from feeling any impulse to exploit me that he felt protective of me."[1]

Common sense, millennia of history, and the Word of God tell us that, except for husband and wife, family members are not meant to be sexual partners.[2] Deuteronomy 27:22 says, "Cursed is the one who has sexual relations with his sister, the daughter of either his father or mother" (NET).[3]

The sibling love that many brothers and sisters share demonstrates that feelings of endearment between members of the opposite sex need not be confused or entangled with sexual attraction. Experience and history attest to this truth about human nature.

This premise begs the next question. If biological brothers and sisters can manage it, can men and women not related by birth or law share an affectionate, yet nonsexual, relationship?[4]

Brothers and Sisters in Christ

We know the sexual norm for families in the home. The vast majority of us have lived it. But what about sexual norms within the church—how Christian men and women treat one another? Can they, too, learn to see one another without the cloud of lust, with pure hearts and eyes?

Learn not to lust? Isn't lust an involuntary reaction for most males when they see an attractive woman? Sumner writes, "Lust is not an innate male reflex; it is a condition of the heart. Lust toward women is not entirely natural. Much of it is learned. How else could it be that men in America tend not to lust for their sisters?"[5]

So yes, we believe that men and women can and should consider one another first as brothers or sisters, as people made in God's image. We will have to reprogram our brains a bit, retrain ourselves to acknowledge the opposite sex first as "Brother! Sister! Person! Worthy of respect!" Only then can we function as a healthy body of Christ, emulating Jesus in our relationships with the opposite sex. Though attractions will happen, they need not rule a person's response to another person. Sexuality is good; lust is sinful.

The Bible includes lust and its related terms—sexual immorality, shameful passions—in several lists of sins.

> Keep thinking about things above, not things on the earth, for you have died and your life is hidden with Christ in God. When Christ (who is your life) appears, then you too will be revealed in glory with him. So put to death whatever in your nature belongs to the earth: sexual immorality, impurity, shameful passion [lust], evil desire, and greed which is idolatry. (Col. 3:2–5 NET)

Believers are encouraged numerous times in Scripture to "put on" the new man and to "put off" the old sins through the power of the Holy Spirit now living inside each one of us (Col. 3:10; 2 Cor. 5:17; Eph. 2:1–10). Lust, which Jesus equates with adultery (Matt. 5:27–28), can be conquered, if the Spirit is invited and allowed to fill a person every day. Both men and women battle against impure thoughts and sexual sin to varying degrees. I (Henry) will speak later directly to the men about strategies to fight inappropriate sexual desires. We will also discuss the way our culture exacerbates the problem of sexual immorality, and strategies that help cultivate a pure thought life. But here we highlight our capability, as reflected in typical brother-sister relationships, of viewing one another through nonsexual eyes.

> **Question:** Do you believe that it is possible for Christian men and women to see each other as siblings?
>
> DAN ALLENDER: The issue seems to be one of power. The sibling category is one good metaphor, but why not also "friendship," "peers," or "fellow servants"? I think that the deeper the relationship between male and female, the less likelihood that power in any form, especially power sexually, will be the primary issue that will redirect the relationship.
>
> RONNA MILLER: It seems that in most institutional structures, boundaries are put in place in order to provide protection, but what they actually do is set up constructive power that then limits the ability to be in caring, mature relationships with one another. That is too limiting. In my experience in working with Dan, the work of our relationship is more about how we choose to care for one another than it is wondering if we are going to trip over a boundary line that is going to be misconstrued or misunderstood.
>
> DAN: I would rather be asking this question: how do we move forward together, to be caring for each other in the process of whatever the tasks are that we are hoping to accomplish together? The call of relationship is always primary, and in one sense it is always the alpha and omega. Whatever the tasks are, they are in between the beginning and the end. Relational maturity has to be the goal.

How we view one another sexually—or not—is just one element of cross-gender relationships. Let's explore how a sibling-like relationship between men and women in the church can benefit leadership. What characteristics of a biological family can we reflect in the church family?

The Benefits of Siblings

Brothers and sisters have an advantage over children without siblings—they are members of a team of peers, give or take a few years.[6] Siblings share similar life experiences involving parents, other siblings, school, sports, friends, and more. Brothers and sisters can be an invaluable resource for one another in facing the challenges of life.

Yes, we all know about sibling rivalry. It's real, it's pervasive, but it's not the last word in sibling relationships. It can be, and often is, overcome. Children are sometimes smart enough to enjoy their siblings instead of continually harassing them. Consider these advantages.

Protection

When I (Kelley) was somewhere between eight and ten years old, a few of my brother's acquaintances—none of whom I knew well—were cutting through our yard to the street behind us when they saw me on our driveway. I'm fuzzy on the details, but I remember that they began to crowd around me, with aggressive body language and words. I—tomboy though I was—began to feel intimidated and nervous. Right about then, my brother came out of the house and sized up the situation. He immediately approached us, pulled me away from the boys, and turned to them. Always a tall kid, he towered over these guys. The gist of his conversation with them: "Leave my sister alone! You mess with her, you mess with me."

The boys left. I goggled at Kevin, who just turned around and stomped back into the house. Perhaps it was adolescent pride preventing him from admitting that he did care about me when so often we clashed. But his actions that day proved that family loyalty trumped petty quarrels.

Likewise, in the church, men and women can act as protectors for one another. We aren't talking about physical protection, necessarily, although that can certainly occur. If a sister in Christ is being confronted by a belligerent church member, her brothers in Christ can—and should—stand beside her in support. Dr. Mark Heinemann, seminary professor, remarks that while "your female colleague has to be able to stand her ground in a healthy way in her work environment, a male colleague needs to indicate solidarity in some way and intervene if the female colleague invites him to."[7]

We can help protect one another's reputations, as well. My (Kelley's) church, Rowlett Bible Fellowship, was a small church with only four staff members. To help protect our reputations, and to guard against any appearance of evil, the staff's unwritten policy prohibited one man and one woman being in the building alone together. When I came on board as the women's ministry director, the other part-time pastors were not always there during my office hours. But the senior pastor worked full-time, so we had to be creative in light of the self-imposed safeguard. Our best solution was to leave the doors to the church wide open, saying in effect that we had nothing to hide, and to have our face-to-face discussions in the open room near those doors. We rarely found ourselves in one another's office without the presence of a third party. I'm not advocating that every ministry adopt such a policy. But whatever your situation, be intentional to protect your sacred sibling.

Alliance

Brothers and sisters can also provide emotional support for one another. Erin chose a certain college because her boyfriend was going there. She didn't plan on them breaking up during the first semester. Feeling sad, lost, and alone, she remembered she had another friend on campus—her older brother. His company in the dining halls, on the way to class, or at social events gave her the comfort and security she had been missing. Why? He was a safe person, one who knew her well and would look out for her best interests. She could trust him to take care of her if something went wrong, to listen to her tales of woe, and help her get through the tough time. He was her brother.

An article about siblings in *Time* magazine concluded by saying, "In a world that's too big, too scary and too often too lonely, we come to realize that there's nothing like having a band of brothers—and sisters—to venture out with you."[8] In the church, we need such brothers and sisters. In sibling-like relationships, founded in purity and love for Christ, men and women can support one another in innumerable ways. We are allies, fighting together to teach, equip, counsel, and love the body of Christ. We cannot succeed alone. We benefit from each other's uniqueness. Because leaders serve a variety of people, a female director or pastor needs her male coworker's perspective. Likewise, a male leader cannot effectively guide women without a woman's point of view. Letting lust steal away the potential rewards of cross-gender friendship is tragic.

Help

"Many hands make light work." Families know the truth of this cliché, especially large families. When siblings band together to tackle a certain task, they benefit in several ways. First, the task gets finished more quickly than if one worked alone. Second, harder tasks become easier.

For example, when I (Kelley) was very young (maybe four or five) my mother still smoked cigarettes. My older brother, Kevin, and I hated the smell. I can remember conspiring with Kevin, who usually was Enemy #1, to ask Mom to quit smoking. We were scared (I don't know why), but we gained courage by approaching her together. We stuttered and stammered out our request, but at least we were able to do it! (Her answer, however, stymied us: "I'll quit smoking when you two quit fighting." Sigh.)

Another benefit of teaming up is that it gives each sibling the opportunity to use his or her gifts and talents. Just the act of sharing a task sometimes reveals hidden abilities. Violet and Dash, the superhero sister and brother in the animated movie *The Incredibles*, were typical snippy, adversarial siblings—until the family gets into major trouble. When a machine gun is fired at them, Violet activates her shield to form a clear protective bubble around herself and

Dash. Dash shouts incredulously, "How are you doing that?" "I don't know," Violet responds. "Whatever you do, don't stop!" he screams. The bullets bounce harmlessly away. Then Dash fulfills the potential in his name, using the bubble to propel his sister and himself to safety by racing away at hyperspeed. Neither of them knew of the value of the other's special power until they worked in concert. Only by teaming up could they save each other.

So it goes in the church. Ministry is all about teamwork. The women's ministry events program is not a one-woman show. The director will be willing, even eager, to share the needs of her ministry with the men in the church to utilize their skills and strengths. At my (Kelley's) church, the annual women's ministry fund-raiser is an all-church garage sale. Are only women involved? Of course not. From the senior pastor to the husbands and sons of our women, all manner of men offer their services as publicists, artists, musclemen, and cashiers.

In a classroom setting, students benefit from a mixed-gender teaching approach. One seminary student expressed his appreciation for his male and female professors in a class evaluation:

> I think it was particularly beneficial to have the course taught by a male and female professor. I enjoyed that so much because each professor has different experiences and perspectives. I think that the team-teaching approach greatly adds to the dynamic of the course as well as models a healthy team approach to ministry. And iron sharpens iron, that was apparent.[9]

Another student wrote:

> I think it is a good balance to have a male and female teaching team, as men and women approach the subject in different ways . . . great class![10]

Insight

Siblings help educate one another about the opposite sex. In a recent study at the University of Texas at Arlington, Dr. William Ickes found that, in general, boys with older sisters or girls with older brothers were less fumbling at getting conversations going with opposite-sex strangers and kept the exchange flowing much more naturally. "The guys who had older sisters had more involving interactions and were liked significantly more by their new female acquaintances," says Ickes. "Women with older brothers were more likely to strike up a conversation with the male stranger and to smile at him more than he smiled at her."[11]

Surely having a sister teaches a guy about purely female experiences—emotional roller coasters, the sometimes crazy effects of menstrual cycles, bad hair days—and acquaints him with their need to talk—not just think—things out. Similarly, women with brothers should recall their fierce competitiveness and desire to win (at anything!), their utter delight at bathroom jokes and noises, the camaraderie they shared with their buddies, and their fascination with pretty girls.

These "inside scoops" into the true nature of boys and girls, all gained through personal experience, contribute to our understanding of one another as adult men and women. This knowledge helps us in dating and marriage, platonic cross-gender friendships, working in teams, and leadership situations.

Take Maria, for instance. Maria's experience with her brother, Derek, was a great help when she joined a church staff. Derek was a very competitive guy, and she remembered his spirited enthusiasm when competing with his buddies, even when it was all in fun. So when Maria attended her first staff meeting, she was not shocked or dismayed when two of the pastors started raising their voices, aggressively interacting to win points for their argument. She understood that they weren't angry at each other, that the issue was not personal, and that they would continue to be great friends. Having a biological brother proved beneficial to Maria when working with her spiritual brothers.

Conflict Management

Siblings also learn valuable peacemaking skills in the family playroom. It starts early! When my (Kelley's) boys were only six and two years old, each had already learned negotiating skills and peacemaking strategies. Nate, the oldest, knew (after many painful encounters) that when he wanted the toy truck that little brother, Jack, was playing with, the best method to getting it was to offer something that Jack valued more. Usually, the plan worked. But if he yanked that disputed toy out of Jack's hand, he got himself a screaming brother—plus some disciplinary consequences. Even Jack, when scolded for hurting Nate, began offering his favorite stuffed lamb in apology—the ultimate peace offering!

Conflict resolution skills are among the most valuable a church staffer or volunteer can possess. The church is a living organism and as such, it changes often, which inevitably leads to conflict—ask any pastor. But imagine a church family that remembered the lessons from their childhood playrooms. Can conflict be more than fighting? Can disagreement spawn healthy conversation and generous hearts? If the Spirit is allowed to lead, then yes, brothers and sisters in Christ can resolve conflict in a godly manner.

Unity

Unity should mark the Christian family and the Christian church, but sibling rivalry has troubled us, literally, since the beginning. In his epic retelling of Genesis, *East of Eden*, John Steinbeck calls sibling rivalry the world's "oldest story." The planet's very first siblings, Cain and Abel, were the very first murderer and murder victim. That's not a very good start for family unity! Steinbeck also reminds his readers that if the story disturbs us, "it must be that we find the trouble in ourselves."[12]

Lesa is the middle child in her family. She idolized her older brother and had a baby sister who followed her everywhere. It was Lesa's sworn duty to protect her with her life. But no matter how much die-for comradeship she felt for her brother and sister, there were always sibling rivalries. When they were yelling, clawing, or poised to spit in the face of the "victim du jour," their mom threatened to lock them in the bathroom, all night if necessary, until they worked it out.

Competing for who's number one is a given in most families. And yet, to become a healthy mature family, most siblings know that their rivalries are childish and need to stop. The same applies to us as brothers and sisters in Christ. The Bible instructs us to put away childish ways as we mature in our faith. First Corinthians 13:11 says, "When I was a child, I talked like a child, I thought like a child, I reasoned like a child. But when I became an adult, I set aside childish ways" (NET).

In many biological families, rivalry only heightens as the years go by, and the stakes are usually much higher than "who gets the last Popsicle." Sadly, the church family is sometimes similar. If you've volunteered in any capacity, you've probably witnessed the competition between ministries for funding, classroom space, Sunday morning announcement "airtime," and the list goes on. It is a good thing to desire for your ministry to grow, but we often want the biggest numbers and the coolest T-shirts. Women's and men's ministries such as Bible studies, leadership boards, and service groups are no exception. It can easily become an "us-versus-them" mentality, smacking of the childish behavior of sibling rivalry.

Visit any preschool playground or sit down at most family dinner tables, and you'll see that sibling rivalry is a hard habit to break. Take a look at nature; many animal siblings take rivalry *dead serious*. For example, as baby sharks develop within the mother shark's womb, the biggest baby shark devours all of his brothers and sisters, ensuring for himself all of the available food resources. Or, did you know that the first baby eaglet that hatches kills all his sibling eaglets by pushing them out from the nest as they come out of their eggs? That way all the food that the mother eagle brings will be only for him.[13] (If you have children, we'd advise against sharing these tales for bedtime stories—they might inspire an older child irritated at a younger sibling.)

As much as we'd like to believe it, *brotherly love* does not come naturally. In fact, from the first set of brothers—Cain and Abel—until now, unfortunately, the reverse seems true; sibling rivalry seems the natural response. That's probably why there are so many instructions in the Bible on how to treat "one another" in our spiritual family. To those of us who are like children around the dinner table clamoring for attention, Paul encourages, "Make every effort to keep the unity of the Spirit through the bond of peace" (Eph. 4:3). To put away our childish sibling rivalries and instead pursue unity may be hard work, but for our church families to function with Christlike maturity, we need input from both our brothers and our sisters.

Jesus himself prayed for the church to be unified. He wanted our unity to show the world his authenticity and the Father's love. This prayer was among the last things he spoke to his disciples, one of his final requests:

> I am not praying only on their behalf, but also on behalf of those who believe in me through their testimony, that they will all be one, just as you, Father, are in me and I am in you. I pray that they will be in us, so that the world will believe that you sent me. The glory you gave to me I have given to them, that they may be one just as we are one—I in them and you in me—that they may be completely one, so that the world will know that you sent me, and you have loved them just as you have loved me. (John 17:20–23 NET)

If the church acted like a family—united in both trials and joys, bound in pure sibling love, treating one another with respect and loyalty, abiding in Christ—imagine our witness to the unbelieving world.

DISCUSSION QUESTIONS

1. If you grew up with siblings, how do you think your relationship with your brothers or sisters has impacted your life?

2. How did growing up with siblings prepare you for conflict and partnering with the opposite sex?

3. If you grew up with opposite-sex siblings, how did that relationship impact your dating or marriage relationships?

4. When your siblings entered into puberty, how did you respond?

5. Do you believe biologically unrelated men and women can learn to see one another first as brothers and sisters rather than sexual beings? Explain your answer.

6. Is lust a natural response or is it learned? How might seeing one another as siblings help us love one another with a pure and holy love?

7. This week, find Bible verses that apply to biological families. In a concordance, look up words like *family*, *brother*, *sister*, *father*, or *mother*. Then apply these verses to your church family. Write out how applying these verses might improve or change the way you treat people with whom you work.

Chapter 5

Creating a Family Ethos for Brothers and Sisters

Lord, what is love?
Love is that which inspired My life,
And led Me to My cross, and held Me on My cross.
Love is that which will make it thy joy to lay down
thy life for thy brethren.
Lord, evermore give me this love.

—AMY CARMICHAEL

Church Ethos

Every place has an ethos. What is ethos? It's the distinguishing tone, environment, or climate—and it's powerful. It impacts how people feel, act, and respond. Maybe you were searching for a church home and you visited church after church—and it just wasn't right. And then you visited a church and it wasn't long before you knew— this is it! You weren't sure why, but you felt at home.

I (Kelley) experienced that "come-home" feeling at Creekside Community Church, to which I was introduced by the guy I was seriously dating. After a few months of warm welcome and acceptance into new friendships, ministry opportunities, and meaningful worship, my dating relationship fell apart. I had to choose—stay in this small church where everyone knew what happened and where I'd see my now ex-boyfriend often, or find a new church home and start over. I chose to stay because I realized I had found a place that was worth more than the short-term hurt. They had become my faith family. That is ethos.

Biological Family Ethos

Every home has an ethos. Some of us were blessed to be born into families where we were cherished, even when we messed up. Others of us knew we were one breath away from words (or hands) that hurt, no matter how hard we tried. If we made an A, they wanted to know why it wasn't an A+. One home is an incubator, the other a deep freeze. The first conjures up warm feelings throughout life that energize their offspring. Children from the deep freeze spend much of their life thawing out and trying to overcome the cold. It has nothing to do with the place's material value or its size. It is something intangible, yet of great consequence—it is ethos.

School Ethos

Every classroom has an ethos, whether it's located in a school, church, or living room. The physical rooms may look almost identical but the teacher or leader sets an atmosphere that profoundly impacts what happens there. In Dr. Hamilton's room we could ask anything—even *stupid* questions. We knew that Dr. Hamilton would never humiliate us—he might challenge us, but we knew his goal was to make us more than we thought we could be. But we all sat silent in Mrs. London's class. It was cold in there, no matter the room temperature. The first time a fellow student asked a question, Mrs. London shut him down with a biting remark. Only the bravest, or the foolhardy, dared venture into dialogue with Mrs. London after that. The ethos forbade it.

Ministry Workplace Ethos

Every workplace has an ethos—including ministry workplaces. The ministry leader, whether volunteer or paid, creates the ethos, intentionally or unintentionally, and that ethos trickles down into every nook and cranny of the ministry.

Georgia micromanaged her children's ministry staff, monitoring every detail, quick with words of rebuke but miserly with praise. Their creativity stifled, her staff began to pick at one another as well as at their volunteer workers. Soon the volunteers started complaining that they needed more rooms, more supplies, and more appreciation. By Christmas three of the four staff were looking for other positions and a third of the volunteers quit, resulting in a pathetic Christmas program that embarrassed everyone in the audience.

Mark hired the best people on his pastoral staff that he could find, and his goal was few turnovers, and then only if they were a poor fit for their ministry. He did not require them to keep office hours. He wanted them to work wherever they were most productive. He provided a comfortable office but if they accomplished more at home or the local Starbucks, all the better. He budgeted money to send each on a yearly mission trip. He wanted the church to develop a global mind-set and knew it started with staff. He insisted each take several days a month and get away for one-on-one time with the Lord. Every seven years, each enjoyed a six-month paid sabbatical to rest, refresh, or focus on a ministry project. Occasionally an e-mail would flash across everyone's screen—"let's go out for ice cream," or "let's go see a movie tomorrow—on me."

Ethos Begins with the Leader

What impacts ethos? Many factors—for example, the depth of the leader's relationship with God; their spiritual, emotional, and mental health; their view of themselves and others; their view of their role as leader; their comfort empowering others; and, if the team is mixed-gender, their view of the other sex.

If you influence others, you create the ethos. Who you are, how you think, and what you believe colors the atmosphere. And what you think and feel about the opposite sex will determine whether or not men and women work together as brothers and sisters. You are responsible for the ministry's health. It all begins with you.

As a leader, what kind of working atmosphere do you want to create? What kind of ministry ethos is optimal for both the men and the women God entrusts to you? First, let's talk in general terms and then we will consider how to create a healthy mixed-gender ethos. As we consider a healthy ethos in general terms, there are two models that we do *not* want to emulate. We are not saying these are bad models in themselves—but they are not appropriate for ministry.

> **What are the advantages of partnering with women in ministry? . . . When you leave out a significant portion of the population and think that you are doing ministry, all you have developed is a structure of patronization. It is a tragedy that we even have to think in these terms.**
>
> —Dan Allender

The Military Model

I (Sue) grew up in a military family, traveling the world, loyal to the red, white, and blue. For thirty years, my father served as a Coast Guard officer. The military has the grave responsibility of protecting our nation from aggressors; its structure must reflect that mandate. Rank, decorum, protocol, and formality are required for the military to be effective in its calling. Walk into a military office and you will sense the unique ethos. "Yes, sir"—"No, ma'am"—"Right away, sir." But the Bible does not instruct ministry leaders to create this formal kind of ethos based on rules and regulations, rank, and protocol. Those of us who love rigid structures and organization sometimes try to impose that model on the church, but an honest look at Scripture does not yield that conclusion. (We will look at biblical examples of how to relate later in this chapter.)

Back in the fifties, my family did not mix socially with enlisted men's families. The workplace was not a place for friendship between *unequals*—and that extended to relationships between nursery

school children. Even as a small child, I remember feeling that this
military rule was unjust and unnecessary. As a result, we created secret play coalitions of military children, sneaking off to enjoy the
forbidden fruit of fellowship, undetected by adults.

My son-in-law, an Air Force pilot, tells me that this particular re-
striction is no longer enforced, opening the way for "mixed" friendships between officers and enlisted personnel. I'm glad to hear of the
change. However, in a military model, there will always be relational
barriers and formal structures, required to defend our country and
fight wars. But not in ministry. Military-style hierarchy that segre-
gates men and women from partnering as equals, as brothers and
sisters in God's family, hurts God's work. We are not saying that sisters should usurp a brother's role as the key leader, but a true brother
does not lord over a sister, in military fashion (Matt. 20:25–28).

The military model impedes the kind of community ethos needed
to build a strong body of believers equipped to fight a different kind
of battle. Spiritual warfare requires camaraderie born in an ethos
that fosters true sibling relationships—the kind that we have already
observed in Jesus and Paul with their "sisters."

The Business/Professional Model

Think of a typical business or professional climate. How do
people relate? What is the purpose of business? The bottom line
is profit. It's all about getting ahead at the expense of competitors.
CEOs build companies, hiring employees to do their bidding.

A business or professional working environment is not personal—
not really. Employees are valuable as long as they are useful to the
company. This does not mean that companies don't care about their
employees. Many have learned that it is in their own best interest to
treat their employees fairly. Otherwise there is too much turnover,
they lose good people, and the bottom line suffers. But companies
are not there to help people—people are there to help the company.

The business/professional model helps create a productive econ-
omy—and there is nothing wrong with that. But ministry is not
about making money or building the biggest building or touting the

largest numbers. It's easy to get confused about that in ministry, especially if the leader is confused about what kind of model to emulate. Ministry is about healing men and women and sending them out for the glory of God. As ministry leaders, we are not called to create a business or professional ethos.

However, the military and the business/professional mind-set still lurks in some minister's minds today. Should a senior pastor be friends with his executive pastor, the youth pastor, the women's minister, the children's director, or his administrative assistant? How should ministry relationships function? What kind of ethos does the Lord want us to create?

> When we sit at the table as colaborers and friends, we have to be careful about the "male locker room" or "female locker room" atmosphere—for men it's punching one another, joking, interrupting each other. Instead when we work together we must be intentional about setting a different tone. Otherwise the men, usually the overwhelming majority, will win out and it's really not a good meeting. I'm intrigued by the concept of sitting together, thinking of each other as family.
>
> —Steve Roese

The Family Model

The Bible uses family imagery to describe ministry relationships. Over and over, Paul addresses his readers as *adelphoi*, traditionally rendered "brothers" or "brethren" or, in the opinion of the NET Bible scholars' gender-accurate language, "brothers and sisters." Our purpose in this work is not to argue the issue of "gender-inclusive" language versus "gender-accurate" language. We simply want translations of the Bible to reflect the original language, without "ideological gender inclusivity." In other words, let's be as close to the original language as we can, without capitulating to anyone's agenda.[1] Whether you translate *adelphoi* as "brothers and sisters" or just "brothers," the point is the same. Paul uses family language repeatedly to address the church.

When Paul describes the ethos he created in the Thessalonian church, he paints a picture of a caring family.

> As apostles of Christ we could have been a burden to you, but we were gentle among you, *like a mother* caring for her little children. We loved you so much that we were delighted to share with you not only the gospel of God but our lives as well, because you had become so dear to us. . . .
> You are witnesses, and so is God, of how holy, righteous and blameless we were among you who believed. For you know that we dealt with each of you *as a father* deals with his own children, encouraging, comforting and urging you to live lives worthy of God, who calls you into his kingdom and glory. (1 Thess. 2:6–8, 10–12, italics added)

And don't forget Paul's instructions to Timothy.

> Do not rebuke an older man harshly, but exhort him as if he were your father. Treat younger men as brothers, older women as mothers, and younger women as sisters, with absolute purity. (1 Tim. 5:1–2)

Worth the Work

We need ministries based on a family model, but instead we usually see business, military, and sports models. Then the emphasis is on who is in charge, who wins, and who is the star. The church becomes competitive, focused on the individual and the bottom line. I don't see these models in the New Testament. Instead we see a community-based family model. It takes both men and women to create a family model.

—Dr. Michael Lawson

We admit that a personal or family ethos is more complicated. It is easier to relate to one another like we're in the military or in business than to relate to one another as family or friends. The lines are clearer; the structure set. Personal relationships require love, peace, patience, kindness, gentleness, self-control—the fruit of the Spirit. They demand wisdom as we create an ethos of care and respect. A family ethos is a supernatural ethos, superintended by the Holy Spirit. But life transformation and exciting spiritual adventure are the norm in a supernatural ethos—and that's the kind of place where Jesus shows up and works wonders. Family ethos has a different feel from military or business models. This model includes friendship, as author Dan Allender explains:

> Leaders disagree about the wisdom of having friends in the organization. Working closely with good friends can create a conflict of interest. That's because a good friend is not merely a person with whom you spend time or share concerns and support. A friendship involves truth, or a pledge of fidelity. The word *troth* comes from the root word that is the same as the word *truth*. Friends make an oath of loyalty to live in truth and/or honor, protect and provide for each other.[2]

When we are true friends, we have one another's best interest at heart. The people we minister with are more important than the task we seek to accomplish together—their welfare, spiritual growth, gift mix, and ministry fit matter.

Did Jesus put projects over people? No. That may be required in some business or military contexts (although soldiers who fight side by side will tell you that they are fighting for their buddies as much as for the cause) but it does not work in ministry. Allender continues,

> Having friends at work can be problematic, and not having friends at work can be problematic. People who avoid friendships at work usually do so because of the uncertainty, fear, and awkwardness of relational intimacy. This leads to a culture that divides the heart from the task, one's

personhood from the work. The bifurcation of head and heart inevitably creates a culture of hiding and manipulative politicizing.[3]

Working friendships bring complications. But healthy ministry requires community—a family serving God together. And friendships between men and women are part of the picture. Loving one another as siblings is not optional if we want to do God's work, God's way— as a spiritual family of friends. If you are a male leader, how you view your sisters has a huge impact on the kind of ethos you create for sisters. It's not just about your ideas on the role of women in ministry. It's about whether or not you see women as sisters, precious and valuable as coworkers with you in ministry. And if you are a woman, your views about men will make or break you in ministry. If you have issues with your father or anger over gender injustices, work them out before you attempt to serve in ministry. Your personal view of men will color how you work with them, and unresolved issues will hinder your capacity to love them as your brothers.

> How does a healthy family function? The best working model is when Mom and Dad work together using their gifts, valuing one another's ideas, and respecting each other in the process. They listen to each other and make better decisions together. As a result, the children feel safer when Mom is empowered and Dad is respectful. The same principles apply in the church. Just as we need both a dad and a mom in the home, we need men and women working together in ministry. When they do, the congregation feels safer and the church thrives.
>
> —Dr. Michael Lawson

The Bible instructs leaders to create a ministry ethos that feels like family. It begins with the leader and trickles down. My (Sue's) senior pastor, Andy, concludes his welcome to newcomers with these words: "Lord, let me do ministry well, and let me do it with my friends." His philosophy has led to the expansive growth of a healthy staff, volunteer teams, and church community. He has created a family ethos, resulting in changed lives and God's glory every day—impacting both men and women. But *how* do we do the same?

The One Anothers

"One another" phrases are used fifty-eight times in the New Testament. They describe a caring and respectful family ethos. They help us live together as a Christlike community, applicable in mixed gender relationships.

Be devoted to one another in brotherly love. (Rom. 12:10)

My (Sue's) kids squabbled constantly, but let someone outside the family lay a hand on one of them—and watch out! That's devotion. How does that look in ministry?

Steve is a great example of a leader who is devoted to his team. When I worked for him, I knew he had my back. He supported me, even when I had blown it. That did not mean that he never confronted me. But never in public—and always for my good. He was a loving friend and brother. If you were not a good fit for his team, he would not leave you there. But, if you were willing to work with him, he would work to help you find the right place.

When leaders are devoted to their teams, they set them up for success. They foster devotion in return, and, again, that attitude trickles down to the whole ministry.

Encourage one another and build each other up. (1 Thess. 5:11)

I (Sue) have two daughters who are natural encouragers. They are gifted with the right words and actions, helping others see what God sees in them. I am not. Instead my natural bent is to be a focused, hard-driving, get-it-done leader. It's easy with that temperament to be on to the next project forgetting to thank and encourage the people who made it happen. It's easy to put programs over people— a tendency I have to fight. I love to accomplish tasks—but I love people more. So I have learned to encourage and build others up. As a leader, it's not optional. It's required if you want to create family ethos that changes lives.

My first semester as a seminary professor, I had not yet taught my butterflies to fly in formation.[4] A note from a younger brother, one of my students, soothed my apprehension and gave me courage to believe that God really had called me to this position.

> I wanted to share with you how much I enjoyed our class today. I want to encourage you and let you know that the interaction was great! Not only did the class time just seem to enjoyably fly by, but we were learning some good practical info! Thank you for taking the time to ask good open-ended questions and encouraging the small group interaction. Integrating those two elements made the presentation of your material quite vibrant.
>
> —Jeremy

His note contained specific examples rather than just nice platitudes. As a ministry leader, your words have amazing impact—probably much more than you realize. For many people, your words are like words from God. Years ago I asked God to enable me to see people's gifts and abilities and then remember to express what I saw. God has done that and it's enabled me to honestly praise people who needed it, whether a sister or a brother.

Greet one another. (Rom. 16:16)

In the early church, men would greet one another by kissing each other on the mouth or both cheeks.[5] Watch men run if we tried that today! For application that works in our time, we must lift a principle out of that culture and translate it into our culture. Today greetings are verbal and physical—a cheery word of welcome, a hearty handshake, a hug, or a slap on the back. For mixed genders, a side hug is appropriate. Whatever form greeting takes, the question is: how do we create an ethos where people genuinely welcome one other? Remember, it all begins with leaders. If they model a lifestyle that reaches out and greets—and if they train their followers to do the same—ministry ethos will warm up.

Do you know why visitors return to a ministry? Is it the great preaching or teaching, the worship, the smorgasbord of programs and activities? No! It all depends on whether or not someone greets them—on whether or not they feel welcome.[6] Haddon Robinson writes, "When people are asked what they look for in a church, their number one response is friendliness. Unfortunately, the reality is that many churchgoers are as distant as a star and as cold as space. . . . In a world where many people couldn't care less, Christians should be people who couldn't care more."[7]

Greeting is a skill and an art. It is unfortunate how many people sign up to be greeters and never greet anyone. Instead, they stand around and talk to their friends. Greeters must be trained. They must learn how to walk up to a stranger and initiate a conversation. It's hard work and it requires stepping out of one's comfort zone. But it's necessary to create a family ethos.

What about greeting someone of the opposite sex? This won't be uncomfortable if you view the other gender as a brother or sister. You are not hitting on them—you are welcoming them to the community. Let's not ignore over half the world as we greet! Develop a ministry mind-set that reaches out and connects, and you will create a family ethos that enables people to relax, heal, learn, and serve—no matter their sex.

Serve one another in love. (Gal. 5:13)

A story from the "greatest generation" encourages us to live out the principle of serving one another in love. Shortly after World War II ended, Europe began rebuilding. Many of the countries were in ruins and one of the saddest sights was the little orphans starving in the streets. Early one chilly morning, an American soldier was returning to his barracks in London when he spotted a little lad with his nose pressed against the window of a bakery. Inside the chef was kneading dough for a fresh batch of scrumptious pastries.

The soldier pulled his jeep to the curb and asked the boy, "Son, would you like some?"

"Boy, would I!"

The soldier stepped inside and bought a dozen of the most delicious, piping hot pastries you've ever tasted, and handed the bag to the boy. As the soldier walked away, he felt a tug on his pants and he turned to hear the child ask, "Mister, are you God?"

God so loved the world that he gave. We are never more like God than when we serve. When my (Sue's) second daughter was born, I battled depression. I did not see how I could care for my eighteen-month-old, and a new baby, and manage a household. Then Mary showed up at my doorstep. She brought a pork roast, mashed potatoes and gravy, a salad she mixed in my kitchen, broccoli with cheese sauce, and a fresh strawberry cake. It was a special delivery from heaven and the food, along with her assuring words, gave me hope. With spiritual mothers and sisters like this around me, I knew I was going to make it.

For me (Sue), serving those of the same gender came naturally, but I was less certain about serving men. What was appropriate? What if they misunderstood my motives? I'm sure many of you can relate. However, as I began to see them as siblings, things changed.

James, a dynamic six-foot African-American pastor, is a guest lecturer in several of our courses. One morning the handouts for his lecture had not been delivered to the classroom, and it was time for him to begin. He started out the door to make the five-minute trek to retrieve them when I stopped him.

"Let me get them for you," I offered.

"Oh, no, I can do it," he responded.

"Please let me. I want to," I insisted.

"No, it's not necessary," he countered.

For some reason, maybe because I am female or his senior by some thirty years, he kept refusing my help. Finally, I looked him in the eye and, with hands on my hips and a smile on my face, bellowed, "Let a sister serve you!" He grinned and nodded. Paul's mandate to serve one another extends to both brothers and sisters—an important way we create a caring family ethos wherever we are.

Accept one another, then, just as Christ accepted you, in order to bring praise to God. (Rom. 15:7)

Biological families are diverse—different ages, genders, personalities, and perspectives. As we observe the amazing differences in families, and all throughout creation, it looks like our Creator God loves diversity. A mark of maturity is appreciating and enjoying variety. Do our ministries reflect God's attitude?

In the first century, the Jerusalem church was the mother church, but the Antioch church was the missionary church. What do you know about their leadership team?

> In the church at Antioch there were prophets and teachers: Barnabas, Simeon called Niger, Lucius of Cyrene, Manaen (who had been brought up with Herod the tetrach) and Saul. (Acts 13:1)

First we note that the team included both Jews and Gentiles. Barnabas, Simeon, and Saul boasted Jewish genealogies while Lucius and Manaen hailed from a Gentile heritage. Culturally, these two groups were miles apart. They did not intermarry or share meals. Paul and Peter sparred over this issue, a conflict that threatened to divide the church.

> When Peter came to Antioch, I [Paul] opposed him to his face, because he was clearly in the wrong. Before certain men came from James, he used to eat with the Gentiles. But when they arrived, he began to draw back and separate himself from the Gentiles because he was afraid of those who belonged to the circumcision group. The other Jews joined him in his hypocrisy, so that by their hypocrisy even Barnabas was led astray. (Gal. 2:11–13)

Paul called Peter on his bigotry, thereby making Christianity more inviting to Gentiles. There must have been challenges as the Antioch leadership team worked together, but they overcame their differences because God called them to minister together. God calls us to do the same today.

The team came from different socioeconomic backgrounds. Manaen had been reared with Herod the Tetrarch. This was Herod Antipas who beheaded John the Baptist and acted so shamefully at Jesus' trial. Manaen grew up in the royal court, undoubtedly an indulgent lifestyle, but he left it behind to follow Jesus.[8] Imagine the differences between Manaen and Herod—one a Christ-follower and the other a Christ-persecutor—the makings of interesting family reunions!

Simeon was called Niger ("black"), which indicates he was of dark complexion. (Tradition says he could be the Simon of Cyrene who carried Jesus' cross, but there is no proof.)[9] Lucius's home was Cyrene, in North Africa, so he probably was dark skinned also. Two black men on the lead team of the first missionary church! Consider the ramifications!

There may have been differences in educational backgrounds among the Antioch leadership team, with Paul, the scholar, who trained in the finest rabbinical schools, and others probably less educated. But despite all these differences, the text indicates that they worked together to serve the Antioch community, creating a home base for Paul and Barnabas, their first missionaries. They planted numerous churches on Paul's three missionary journeys.

Paul wrote, "Accept one another . . . in order to bring praise to God." Although women were not listed as the key leaders in Antioch, based on our observations of Jesus' and Paul's interaction with women as sisters, we believe women were active ministry partners there.

Men and women are called to accept one another in order to bring praise to God too! If you are a man, do you appreciate the way God designed women, or do you secretly feel superior? The same question applies to women. It takes intentionality and hard work to appreciate and enjoy people who are different from us—culturally, racially, ethnically, socioeconomically—and to esteem the opposite sex. But just as the church was strengthened by diversity in Antioch, it will be strengthened today as men and women value one another's contributions and work together as siblings.

Be completely humble and gentle; be patient, bearing with one another in love. (Eph. 4:2)

Create an ethos where people can be open about their struggles and get real help. We are not saying be soft on sin or pamper people, but we are all in-process and need mercy. How sad when couples leave the church to divorce and no one even knew they were having problems! We must create an ethos where people can be open and real.

I (Sue) love to train teachers and Jackie was one of the women I helped. I remember her first message. It was her life story and I was helping her prepare. She did not grow up a Christian and some of her teen escapades do not make polite conversation. She was planning to tell the women about the little devil tattooed on her hip. She explained that each day as she was getting dressed, she thanked God for the transformation in her life—that she was no longer under the power of the enemy. As I listened to her rehearse, part of me wanted to nix the part about the devil on the hip. I envisioned proper ladies with raised eyebrows. But another part of me wanted to leave it in. I prayed and God led me to hold my tongue. After Jackie spoke, many women felt the freedom to talk about their hidden tattoos as well as their struggles, problems, and sins that needed to be exposed to heal. Today Jackie is an exceptional Bible teacher.

As with earlier "one anothers," many of us are more comfortable bearing with those of the same gender. Can we create an ethos where we also bear with the opposite sex? Paul's admonition in Ephesians 4:2 is aimed at everyone bearing with everyone—not just those of the same sex!

Marilyn's husband, Bob, traveled three weeks a month. She confided in me that she was overwhelmed caring for their three children, all under the age of five. She battled a bitter spirit every time he came home. She especially resented him stepping in as disciplinarian, often in contrast to her methods. I understood her frustration but was grieved when I observed how she disagreed with him in front of the children.

Marilyn administered her youngest daughter's yucky antibiotic with a jelly bean chaser. When their middle son clamored for a jelly bean too, Bob firmly told him, "No, you can't have one now. Wait until after dinner." But Marilyn flippantly remarked, "Yes, you can," and gave him the jelly bean before Bob could protest. He walked away in silence and spent the evening behind a newspaper.

The next week Marilyn and I talked about the interchange. She admitted it was disrespectful, an expression of her bitter spirit. She also confessed that Bob did not enjoy traveling but since he had been laid off two years ago, this job was all he could find to support the family. He was looking for work that allowed him to be the dad and husband he desired. But for now he needed her support. Husbands are brothers too! Healthy families, both biological and spiritual, bear with one another.

Invisible Influence

Ethos is invisible—but it can make or break a ministry. You can create an ethos that feels like family. The Bible tells us how: be devoted to one another and encourage, greet, serve, accept, and bear with one another. When we do, we will also create a place where men and women love one another and serve together as brothers and sisters—a radical transformation that just might turn the world upside down for Jesus.

DISCUSSION QUESTIONS

1. What is ethos? Describe both positive and negative family, school, and workplace ethos.
2. If you have served in the military, how would you describe its ethos? Have you observed anyone imposing a military model on the church? If so, how did it look and feel? (No names, please.)

3. Do you know of ministries that look more like businesses? (No names, please.) How did they look and feel?
4. Review 1 Thessalonians 2:6–8, 10–12. What kind of ethos did Paul foster in the church at Thessalonica?
5. Name some advantages of a family model in ministry.
6. What tensions can you envision when a ministry attempts to create a family ethos?

Chapter 6

Brothers and Sisters:
The Same, Only Different

There was a perfect man who met a perfect woman. After a perfect courtship, they had a perfect wedding. Their life together was, of course, perfect. One snowy, stormy Christmas Eve this perfect couple was driving along a winding road when they saw someone in distress. Being the perfect couple, they stopped to help.
There stood Santa Claus with a huge bundle of toys. Not wanting to disappoint any children, the perfect couple loaded Santa and his toys into their car. Soon they were driving along delivering toys. Unfortunately, the driving conditions deteriorated and the perfect couple and Santa Claus had an accident. Only one of them survived.
Who was the survivor?

The Female Response? The perfect woman. She's the only one that really existed in the first place. Everyone knows there is no Santa Claus and there is no such thing as a perfect man.
The Male Response? So, if there is no perfect man and no Santa Claus, the perfect woman must have been driving. This explains why there was a car accident.

GENDER WRANGLING! Men and women poking seemingly harmless fun at each other. Women say men are like lava lamps—fun to look at, but not all that bright. Men ask, "What do you call a smart blonde?" and answer "a golden retriever." Usually these jokes are based on stereotypes.

A Complex Subject

When I (Sue) studied for my doctorate (2000–2004) in Boston, my professors taught us that gender research is muddy, assumptions are difficult to prove, and in reality few differences between the sexes had actually been documented. Between lectures, my classmates—all women—would gather to banter the issue. Some agreed with the professors while others would argue the opposite perspective over dinner—for hours. *No, men and women* are *different species,* they would insist, *an unbridgeable gap separates us.*

The same debates continue on the campus where I teach, sometimes giving men and women a pass for objectionable behavior or excuses to limit opportunities. "Men are hardwired to find purpose in their work. We can't expect them to be too involved in their families." "God designed women to be detailed. They can't lead effectively because they don't see the big picture." Those kinds of statements may sell books, but do they really help men and women navigate through complex life issues? Those kinds of statements bother us.

In this chapter, we present varied and contradictory perspectives on gender differences. It's a thorny subject, and intelligent people with good motives draw different conclusions. Our intention is to lay out pieces of the puzzle for you to consider as you form your own opinion related to differences between people of the opposite sex. As you do so, keep in mind the caution of one counselor: "It is important for us to remember that averages reported about groups cannot give us reliable information about specific individuals."[1]

It's Personal

The issue of gender differences is very personal for many, impacting our identity. For example, I (Sue) never fit the female cookie cutter.

I doubt you could tell by looking. I'm feminine in demeanor and dress, but on gift and ministry style tests, I score off the charts as a leader. Put me in a group and in time I'm usually out in front. I love to challenge the group to their best for God—it's the way God designed me. I accept and enjoy this about myself now, but for years I thought there was something wrong with me. Why? Because I was taught by well-meaning men and women that leadership was masculine. Whether you fit the "mold" or not, remember that many of your spiritual siblings struggle with it. The topic deserves *all* our attention.

The Human Element Impacts Research

I (Sue) have read books on the topic of gender differences authored by scientists, public policy experts, family therapists, medical doctors, and professors of behavioral neuroendocrinology and psychology. Many begin by explaining the opposing view and promise to be fair to both sides, but many renege, their agenda emerging as they write. They ultimately choose sides in the tug-of-war. Dr. M. Gay Hubbard writes:

> In reviewing gender studies, the reader soon discovers that he or she must try to identify the often unstated value system of the researcher which has shaped the way in which the research has been reported.
>
> It is a myth to believe that science is carried out by rational, objective searchers for truth, who are uninfluenced by the world around them. Scientists, like other humans, are deeply influenced by their belief system and the environments in which they work.[2]

Make sure to remember the human element as you evaluate gender studies.

Two Camps

Historically, sociologists, psychologists, scientists, educators, and theologians have divided into two camps—the nature camp and the nurture camp. The nature camp argues that gender differences are innate. Many present a cookie-cutter picture of each sex: women are _____; men are _____. You fill in the blanks. They don't seem concerned that stereotyping hurts those who don't match their preconceived views of masculinity and femininity.

The nurture camp insists that differences between men and women are learned, and if we change the environment, we can eliminate them. This perspective ignores the glaring differences I see between my grandchildren—Caleb, who hurls the ball at me in an endless, gleeful game to see which comes first, smacking Grandma or breaking something—and Becca, who sits in the corner engrossed in making up stories with her family of plastic horses. And these differences were apparent before Caleb knew he was a boy and Becca knew she was a girl. The controversy continues, but we wonder if new discoveries, especially about the functioning of male and female brains, may ultimately break the stalemate. Advancements in the ability to actually compare male and female brains in action challenge both the nature and nurture camps—those who insist the differences are hardwired and impenetrable, and those who insist no meaningful differences exist. Save us from both extremes! New research may be the catalyst for many Christians to find middle ground.

As we will observe later in the chapter, research is discovering evidence that supports the idea that God created men and women innately different. The "different" camp was right. But before you nature lovers dance a victory jig, we will also see that science has revealed that many of your assumptions about men and women that led to stereotyping were wrong too. Note what Dr. Hubbard points out:

The first sex and gender study which most of us remember is in Mother Goose—it reports distinct differences between boys and girls. "What are little girls made of?" asks the old nursery rhyme. The answer is quite positive: "Sugar and spice and everything nice . . ." In contrast, the description of little boys reflects a clearly gender-biased view: "Frogs and snails and puppy dog tails, that's what little boys are made of."

Present research both confirms and denies the old nursery rhyme. The answer to the question, "Are men and women different?" appears to be, "Yes, but . . . not as much as we once thought, and often in ways quite different than we once assumed."[3]

> My wife, Carolyn, stresses what she calls the "Blessed Alliance," that is, men and women working together for the cause of Christ. When we look at Genesis, we find that the first team God put together was not male and male, or female and female, but male and female. Their job was to "rule and subdue the earth" together.
>
> As seminary president, I actively recruit women for seminary training alongside the male seminarians. Men and women preparing side by side for ministry will have long-term benefits for the church. In this way, I believe seminaries can play a vital role in shaping future ministry.
>
> I would add that men and women are different and bring a different perspective to life problems, to ministry, as well as to the study of the Bible. I find that my ministry partnerships with women greatly enhance my ministry as a seminary president. Frankly, I would not be an effective president or professor without the strong partnership of females.
>
> —Dr. Frank James

Brothers and Sisters Created in the Image of God

If we shed our agendas and pursue intellectual honesty, this new research may help us understand each other and value what each brings to the table. And these new findings may complement biblical revelation. The Bible tells us that both brothers and sisters are made in the image of God.

God created mankind in his own image, in the image of God he created them, male and female he created them. (Gen. 1:27 NET)

In their book *Intimate Allies*, Dan Allender and Tremper Longman ponder the implications this verse has for male-female relationships:

> What an awesome privilege—to reflect, as finite beings, the infinite, perfect beauty of God. And we are able to do so only in the complexity and distinctiveness of both sexes. Both men and women are made in the image of God. Both are necessary to reflect God; one alone is not only incomplete but also inadequate to reflect [God's] glory.[4]

What if God designed us to partner together in the home *and* in the church? Thus, without our partner we are like a single parent, struggling with the overload and overlooking what comes natural to our sibling. We believe it takes both genders to pull off God's work well. Without both, the picture is incomplete and deficient.

Valuing Our Unique Design

How can we all come to a place in our hearts and minds where we value our brothers and sisters, not seeing them as less but as God-designed complements to "the way God made me"? God, the Great Artist, uses a rich, vibrant, and varied palette of colors to paint his picture of home and ministry. Yet so many artists today, because of gender confusion, only dab their brushes in familiar colors, with drab and dull results. To shed our agendas and change our prejudices, we need to look deeper into the conflicting perspectives of gender differences.

Remember . . . the Peril of the Pendulum

In the 1980s, I (Sue) studied under Dr. Howard Hendricks, now a colleague. He taught his students an unforgettable lesson—the peril of the pendulum—a phrase that applies to our current discussion on gender differences. He impressed us with the truth that there is often serious danger if we go to extremes. As I analyze most of the authors I read on gender differences, perhaps their error is in taking their convictions to extremes: either, *there are no differences between the sexes*, or, *the differences are fixed so match up or you're a misfit.* Often Satan's tactic is to distort God's good gifts, making them evil in extremes. Take food, sex, stuff, work, or leisure. In their place and in good measure, each is beneficial, part of God's blessing and a balanced healthy lifestyle—but go overboard and you are in trouble. Perhaps both nature and nurture are true, unless taken to extremes. What can we learn from extremists' mistakes, enabling us to partner effectively with brothers and sisters in God's work?

Extreme Nature Ideology

While contributing major advances in important doctrines, many early church fathers were extreme proponents of what today is called the nature camp, believing God created women inferior to men. As a result, we find Tertullian (ca. 225) describing women as "the gateway of the Devil . . . the unsealer of the forbidden tree . . . the first rebel against the divine law." He blamed women's nature and held them responsible for making the death of Jesus necessary.[5]

Augustine also held a low view of women. Perhaps his promiscuous early life and ongoing sexual struggles may have played into his formation of that view. He did not consider women to be creatures of reason or capable of understanding. He believed a woman could only learn through following the example of her husband, and because of a woman's seductive nature, she could not be trusted as a teacher. According to Augustine, the only teaching role for a woman was motherhood.[6]

Even Luther joined the male "nature" chorus, expounding, "Take women from their housewifery . . . and they are good for nothing . . . If women get tired and die of bearing, there is no harm in that; let them die as long as they bear; they are made for that."[7]

Doctors in the Victorian era warned women that if they expanded their minds through too much scholarly study, their ovaries would shrink, leaving them infertile and incapable of the function for which they had been placed on earth.[8] For centuries in the extreme nature camp, women simply were less—less intellectually, rationally, ethically, and physically. And that reasoning continues in the minds of some men and women today—to lesser and greater degrees, outright and secretly.

If we harbor these views about sisters *or brothers* in our heads or hearts, we hinder our ability to partner with our siblings, limiting our effectiveness.

Extreme Nurture Ideology

Extremism is just as prevalent on the other side of this issue. In the 1960s many radical feminists imposed their nurture ideology on the West—*insinuate differences and you are a bigot!* Political correctness. Their goal was androgyny—*we are all the same.*[9] As a result, particularly in secular settings, men and women who dared encroach into the danger zone of gender differences risked censorship, or worse.

In an episode of the sitcom *The Simpsons*, titled "Girls Just Want to Have Sums," Principal Skinner is giving a speech at an elementary school assembly (for non-Simpsons fans, Skinner is almost always politically *in*correct). He unfortunately veers into the danger zone of the difference between boys and girls, and as usual, says the wrong thing, resulting in hurled tomatoes and boos.

> "Boys are better at math and science, the real subjects. I don't know why girls are worse."

Later in the episode, he tries to appease the women by calling for a diversity forum, in which he says a few other choice lines.

> "I understand the problems of women." [*Pause.*] "Women are unique in every way." [*Again pause.*] "Ah . . . it is the differences, of which there are none, that make the sameness exceptional."

He drawls on, and finally as the audience is on the brink of bedlam, Skinner exclaims, *"Just tell me what to say!"*[10]

The days of gender political correctness are still with us, resulting in many of us wanting to throw up our hands in frustration like Principal Skinner, "Just tell me what to say!" But those days may fade as discoveries shed new light on the workings of male and female brains.

Research Breakthroughs

Extreme nurture ideology may wane due to the intervention of science and medical technology. For example, MRI scans show male and female brains in action—and the results defy the "no difference" crowd. Men's and women's brains *are* intrinsically different, but *not* in ways that please many in the nature camp. We'll turn next to take a brief look at some of the new research—the findings sent some social and medical scientists reeling. But first listen to recent comments by two authors. The first is by Doreen Kimura, who wrote *Sex and Cognition*.

Most of us have grown up with brothers and sisters who have shared most aspects of our environment, yet we turned out quite different. We all have friends with backgrounds similar to our own, yet here the diversity in temperament, skills, and ultimate occupation is often greater. A social scientist flatly unwilling to entertain the idea that there are important biological contributions to the variations we see in cognitive pattern from one person to another has stopped being a scientist and has become an ideologue. It has been suggested that a distinguishing characteristic of ideology is its commitment to a position, regardless of evidence (Hilborn 1996). Sexism, racism, and egalitarianism can all be considered ideologies to the extent that they are commitments to a system of beliefs without empirical support.[11]

Leonard Sax, a graduate of MIT and the University of Pennsylvania, a medical doctor and a psychologist, has entered the debate with his book *Why Gender Matters.*

On the same bookshelf you can find books that do affirm the existence of innate differences in how girls and boys learn. But what books! Books with titles like *The Wonder of Boys* and *Girls Will Be Girls* promote antiquated and inaccurate gender stereotypes. "Girls are more emotional than boys." "Boys have a brain-based advantage when it comes to learning math." As we'll see, those familiar notions turn out to be false.

On one hand, you have books claiming that there are no innate differences between girls and boys, and that anybody who thinks otherwise is a reactionary stuck in the 1950s. On the other, you have books affirming innate differences between girls and boys—but these authors interpret these differences in a manner which reinforces gender stereotypes.

These books have only one thing in common. They are based less on fact—and more on their author's personal beliefs or political agenda—either to deny innate sex differences, or to use sex differences in child development as a justification for maintaining traditional sex roles.[12]

Now, let's look at some of the recent research results that argue for differences between men and women. We believe these differences do not limit or devalue either son, but they are differences ordained by God to help us complement one another as we work side by side as brothers and sisters.

Divinely Designed Counterparts

In the late 1800s, scientists discovered that the left side of the human brain seemed to be specialized for language and the right side for spatial intelligence. For decades, because almost all subjects of the research were male, this concept was assumed to be true for both men and women. You may have been taught this "fact." Maybe you still believe it?

In 1964 scientists began to ask whether there are anatomic differences in the way male and female brains function. Through research on stroke victims, they found that although the left hemisphere of the brain is clearly specialized for language function in men, women's brains are not as compartmentalized. Women use both hemispheres of their brain for language while men primarily use the left.[13]

Before you begin hypothesizing on what this means for the behaviors of both sexes—*men are less verbal, women can multitask*—be careful. No one knows for sure. You may be embarking down the yellow brick road of gender stereotyping. People have a long history of misinterpreting research to promote gender stereotyping, usually at the expense of females.

For example, one hundred years ago, Paul Julius Möbius, a German physician, wrote a best-selling pamphlet entitled *Regarding the Physiological Weak-Mindedness of Women.*[14] He asserted that women's brains were 8–10 percent smaller than men's, even after accounting for body size. He assumed that intelligence was dependent on brain size and used his research to "prove" that males were intellectually superior to females. What he did not know is that women have higher blood flow to the brain per gram of tissue; they have larger cells in critical areas of the brain; and they use the most advanced area of the brain, the cerebral cortex, more than men. Actually, Möbius was correct about brain size indicating intellectual superiority if he had confined his conclusions to men. Males with high IQs do, on average, have slightly larger brains than men with lower IQs. But the findings are not true for women with higher and lower IQs.[15] It's complicated—this brain business—and we must be careful.

But we do know beyond all doubt that male and female brains are different, and it looks more and more like these differences are genetically programmed, present at birth.[16] One is not better. One is not worse. Men and women are both able to accomplish almost all tasks—they simply go about accomplishing them differently. Sax presents a crystal clear analogy of being different, but not better.

The bottom line is that the brain is just organized differently in females and males. The tired argument about which sex is more intelligent or which sex has the "better" brain is about as meaningful as arguing which utensil is "better," a knife or a spoon. The only correct answer is "Better for what?" A knife is better than a spoon if you want to cut through a piece of meat, while a spoon is better if you're facing a bowl of chicken broth.[17]

Consider the research conclusions below.

- Girls' hearing is substantially more sensitive than boys', especially in the 1,000- to 4,000-Hz range, and these differences increase with age. Women probably hear better than men.[18]
- The male retina is substantially thicker than the female retina because the male cells have mostly larger, thicker M cells, while the female retina has predominately smaller, thinner P ganglion cells. As a result, girls see rich textures and variances in colors while males are not as sensitive to these variances and are more drawn to motion. Researchers at Cambridge University found that girl babies would respond first to a young woman's face while boy babies looked first at a mobile. Boys and girls may prefer particular kinds of toys based on the way they see.[19]
- Women typically navigate using landmarks while men are more likely to use absolute directions like north and south. Neuroscientists have learned that the different genders use different areas of the brain when navigating. Females use the cerebral cortex and males use the hippocampus, a nucleus deep inside the brain that is not activated in most women's brains during navigational tasks.[20]
- A Harvard study using MRI imaging sought to understand how emotion is processed in the brains of children. Children process emotions in the amygdala, a primitive area deep

in the brain far from the cerebral cortex where language is processed. Seven-year-olds often can't tell you why they are feeling sad. But as girls mature, brain activity associated with emotion moves out of the amygdala and into the cerebral cortex—in girls, but not in boys. In fact, even in adult men, much of the brain activity associated with emotion remains in the amygdala, making it difficult and uncomfortable for many men to verbalize their feelings.[21]

■ Boys and girls assess risk differently, with boys more likely to report feeling exhilarated by the possibility of danger, whereas girls were far more likely to report feeling fearful. Boys systematically overestimated their own ability while girls were more likely to underestimate their abilities. And a boy was much more likely to do something dangerous when he was in a group than when he was alone.[22]

■ Boys fight twenty times as often as girls do, but after fighting boys usually end up better friends and are more likely to play together. Girls seldom fight, but when they do bad feelings last.[23]

■ On average, girls are better at some aspects of math ability and boys are better at others. Throughout the school years, girls tend to get better scores on the calculation and computation parts of aptitude tests, and boys on the parts requiring mathematical problem solving.[24]

■ Women tend to make moral decisions on the basis of who it might help and who it might hurt. Men tend to make moral decisions on the basis of right and wrong, regardless of how it impacts others.[25]

Can we trust these conclusions? We must be cautious, looking for patterns over time. A number of these studies seem to be backed up by multiple researchers. But do these scientists have hidden agendas? We don't know. At the very least they raise interesting possibilities and questions. Bottom line—they tell us that what we assumed in the past may not be true. These studies indicate that there probably are real differences between the sexes, but not in ways many assumed.

If you tend to follow the nature camp, don't use differences like Augustine and Luther used them—to limit women. None of the differences make either gender less valuable or important. What they highlight is that brothers and sisters need each other. Understanding the beautiful and diverse way God created each sex should send us on a crusade to gain insight into our sacred siblings.

Remember also that some of these findings, like the way boys and girls see, are physical characteristics of all boys and all girls, all men and all women. But most of the findings are not that universal. They are much more difficult to measure and there are great differences *within* the sexes as well as between the sexes.

I'm no scientist, but I do know that there are differences between men and women. But when you stop and look at the broader "differences" picture, there are often major differences within the same gender. I have two sons, and while they may be from the same gene pool they are polar opposites. One wears khaki shorts and button downs; the other wears jeans and skater T-shirts. One is an engineering major at a huge university and the other attends a small liberal arts college in the mountains. But no one ever thinks it's a "Class A" miracle that they get along great and will do about anything to be together.

It seems that people use the differences of men and women to give up on there ever being a working solution. But as I said, no one thinks it strange when members of the same gender differ but still find common ground to make their relationship work. My younger sister and I are extremely different. Growing up, she hid away in her room curled up with a book. I was outside assembling tree forts and gathering ammo for the ensuing battle with the neighborhood "thugs." But even though we are different—and as adults, we live across the country from one another,

> are both busy pastors' wives, moms, and have careers—
> we are inseparable with weekly phone calls and at least
> twice-a-year girl weekends away. We've simply worked on
> our differences.
>
> The Bible uses the metaphor of a family to describe the
> church, in which followers of Christ are to be like mothers, fa-
> thers, sisters, and brothers to one other. This means a healthy
> functioning—working out the differences—kind of family.
>
> —Lesa Engelthaler

We must guard against pigeonholing any of God's unique cre-
ations. At the same time it is foolish to ignore systematic similarities
that can help us value, enjoy, and teach the genders. The peril of the
pendulum! God did not create us male and female so we could tease
or limit one another, but so that we could join together, two images
of God combined to make a whole, and glorify him through our
unity. We are brothers and sisters called to work side by side. More
bonds us than divides us.

Our Mutual Assignments as Brothers and Sisters

Each of us comes into this world with advantages and disadvan-
tages. Some of us arrived to godly, loving parents; others of us were
unwanted. Some of us may have enjoyed an Ivy League education,
while our neighbor had to work to get through community college.
God ordained the century, country, and family into which we were
born (Acts 17:26). He gave us our natural abilities, gift-mix, temperament, and personality. And he determined whether we would be
male or female. Despite the differences, as Christian brothers and sisters we are called to the same ultimate pursuits and responsibilities.

We Are All Called to Know Jesus

Salvation means saved *for* a purposeful life now and *from* eternity
without God. When we trust Christ for salvation, we were born into
God's spiritual family. We are brothers and sisters, with an obliga-
tion to love and treat one another respectfully.

We Are All Called to Grow Up

Sanctification is the process of growing to maturity as we journey through life. The Bible tells us who Christ wants us to be and how he wants us to behave. The fruit of the Spirit (Gal. 5:22–23) is not pink or blue, but applies to both men and women, despite their natural bents because of innate sexual qualities. Men may naturally be more aggressive than women but we are all called to peace and gentleness. Women may be considered more prone to gossip, but all are called to benefit others with their words. Jesus mastered the art of loving others, the model for us all.

We Are All Called to Share Life's Tasks

Have you heard that all women want is security and all men want is significance? It is not true. Yes, security is important to women, and men find great pleasure in meaningful work. And many women, because of their temperaments and gift-mix, enjoy a behind-the-scenes role, but many women do not. They want to participate in "ruling and subduing" beyond their own white picket fence.[26] When men and women attempt to fill a prescribed role that does not fit their gift-mix and design, expect trouble. Let each individual pursue tasks that line up with the way God created them, employing wise priorities, and keeping a good conscience before the Lord.

Parenting is an obvious example of the necessity of men and women to work together in life's tasks. That level of partnership— male and female—is equally necessary in the life of the church, to do an effective job of carrying out our tasks there.

We Are All Called to Obedience

Following Christ means obeying him and making moral decisions based on the Bible. Research suggests that men tend to make moral decisions based on right and wrong, a concern for justice, and women tend to make moral decisions based on how it impacts others, a compassionate perspective.[27] However, women cannot use their natural tendencies as an excuse to make unbiblical choices. Maybe God created us this way as brothers and sisters, expecting that we would consult one another, dialogue, and hammer out tough decisions together based on both right and wrong *and* how the decision impacts others—justice and compassion. Consider how this process might result in wise family and ministry decisions for both future generations and God's work on earth. As Dan Allender reminds us,

> Honest hunger after truth requires us to remain open to everyone, including those with whom we disagree and have conflict. It also requires that we remain open to the fact that we desperately need the very people who challenge and contradict our cherished notions of truth. We may never agree, nor do we need to do so, but we need others—especially those who challenge us to dig deeper and become more human. The hunger, then, is not so much for agreement on factual accounts, but more for truth that leads to greater delight in the truth.[28]

We Are All Called to Serve

Men and women, brothers and sisters, are gifted and empowered by the Holy Spirit to impact their families, churches, and communities—locally and worldwide. Women have all the gifts that men have, and a failure to develop them is criminal. Brothers who lead carry a grave responsibility to see that their sisters have opportunities to equip and serve. Leading means opening doors for those coming alongside, rather than being the boss—a worldly, unbiblical concept. God made us different because we are designed to complement one another in the home and in ministry. Our combined strengths make us a formidable team.

Vive la Différence!

Yes, we are different—and we are the same. Fleshly people use the differences to stereotype, to excuse bad behavior, to put down, to gain advantage, to have their own way. But spiritual people, Christian brothers and sisters, are called to higher ground. Recent breakthroughs have shown us that many of us were wrong in our approach to gender differences. Scientists are quick to say that they have only scratched the surface. There is so much more they do not know and may never know. It's a complex business. Maybe all sides were foolish to be so dogmatic. Maybe one caution for us all is that we need to lay aside our arbitrary assertions, acknowledging that gender differences are a profound mystery.

One thing we know for sure is that our Father calls us to work together—unity not uniformity, respecting and loving each other, complementing one another's individual strengths and weaknesses—for his glory and work on earth.

DISCUSSION QUESTIONS

1. Finish these statements: women are _____; men are _____. These statements reflect stereotypical ideas prevalent in our culture. In your opinion, how accurate are these stereotypes?

2. Are stereotypes harmless or harmful? Explain your answer.

3. Do you agree or disagree with Allender and Longman's quote on page 99? Support your thinking.

4. Many early church fathers exhibited a low view of women. How do you think these ideas influence men and women today?

5. Respond to the recent scientific findings on gender differences. What study was particularly significant to you and why?

6. In your opinion, are men and women more similar than different, or more different than similar? How might your answer impact the way you see your spiritual siblings?

Chapter 7

For Sisters' Eyes Only

We are family,
I got all my sisters with me.
We are family,
Get up ev'rybody and sing.

—SISTER SLEDGE

(GUYS, IT'S OK IF YOU READ THIS TOO.)

Julie's law practice paid the bills, but sometimes she felt her work lacked purpose. Becoming a follower of Jesus a year ago had changed her life immeasurably. Finally she had a family—a faith family—to do life with. Now she wanted her expertise to further the Lord's work. When the pastor announced the start-up of a new inner-city church, Julie knew that it was the perfect place to use her training and experience. In fact, many of her law practice clients were from that area of town, and her legal background might come in handy. She was ready to scale back her hours and invest her time volunteering.

Nine people showed up for the first planning meeting. Associate pastor Randy chaired the meeting, asking Jim to pray and Jeff to give a report on the status of their plans. Although five women attended, Julie noticed that they said little, even though they seemed attentive and excited about the project. She interjected an idea, but her comment was ignored. In the legal world, she was respected, participating in decisions with lawyers, judges, and clients. And yet Julie sensed that in her new faith family, the rules were different and she wasn't sure what they were. Her enthusiasm crushed, she left the meeting wondering if there was a place for her on this project.

Unfortunately, the majority of this ministry team did not contribute their insight, experience, and perspectives to the plans for the inner-city church. If over half of the people reached through this new ministry is female, and statistics say it is,[1] then the project will suffer. What happened? Why didn't the women speak up? Did the brothers mean to exclude their sisters? Was failing to respond to Julie's comment intentional? Sometimes that happens. But just as often, it is an oversight—or the women shut themselves down. They are confused and don't want to appear overbearing. Or sometimes a woman decides to force her way into the process, coming on so strong it is counterproductive. Often, brothers and sisters feel this tension on a mixed-gender team.

How could these nine people—five women and four men—come together, bringing both a masculine and a feminine perspective to benefit the project? What are the "rules" for women working on a mixed-gender team? (Men, we will address your "rules" in the next chapter.)

Jesus' contact with sisters can help women discern healthy ways to figure out this complicated business of relating to men as brothers. Let's look at some principles right out of the New Testament.

Sisters, Speak Up

Many women, for a variety of reasons, are indirect in spelling out what they need or want. For example, of the graduates of Carnegie Mellon University with a master's degree in a business-related field,

male graduates earn, on average, 8 percent more than female graduates. But why? Research shows that the men asked for more money.
During the job-finding process only 7 percent of the women asked for
a larger starting salary compared to 57 percent of the men. The gender gap in salary would have closed if the women had only asked.[2]
    I (Sue) teach seminary classes, both mixed-gender and all female.
In the mixed-gender classes women students are quieter, but these
same students participate heartily in my all-women courses. I see
the same phenomenon in Sunday school. Many women speak up less
when men are present.

> **Question:** How do women change the dynamics of
> meetings?
>
> **Response:** A certain perspective is automatically not go-
> ing to be heard in the same way if a woman's voice is
> not there. It does not mean that a man will not come up
> with the same conclusion or decision that a woman would
> make. But there is something profoundly unique that only
> a woman's voice and perspective can bring.
>
> For instance, if there is some dissension around a staff
> issue taking place at a leadership level, she may be the
> one who sees a dynamic of power differently than a man
> might see it, and she may be able to advocate in a differ-
> ent way or add explanation or clarification into something
> otherwise unheard or unconsidered. It is going to be a
> unique lens only she can bring.
>
> That can be a difficult and dangerous place for the
> woman who is constantly doing such. It doesn't mean she
> has something profoundly different to say at every meeting,
> but she brings an awareness that mirrors what I would hope
> for all of us, institutionally and in every realm as we move
> forward—that there would be an increasing acknowledg-
> ment that a woman's viewpoint can begin to break down
> some of these long-standing structures of power.

> Oftentimes the lens that a woman brings slows things down and means that issues have to be looked at a little differently; steps that have been flown through then become more muddled somehow. The temptation for women is to say, "Oh, good grief, I am just messing this up again. I should have kept quiet, because now we are going to have to rethink this whole issue; now I have upset people."
>
> So much of the learning curve is to acknowledge that what we see, and how we talk about what we see, is actually worth the effort, and acknowledging that we might be met with resistance and misunderstanding. Then begins the work to educate and help others understand why that viewpoint is valuable. It takes work, and some days are much easier than others. This is where women's relationships with other women are so important: it is the conversation that I have with other women, some within and others without, that will validate my voice.
>
> —Ronna Miller

I also observe unhealthy female communication patterns as I counsel wives. Some expect husbands to read their minds. They manipulate and they persuade with lengthy, wordy arguments, when all they need to do is come right out and say it. Many of us have been taught that it is more feminine to be quiet and indirect—to stay in the background. Manipulative and indirect practices hinder good communication between brothers and sisters in ministry work places, and frustrate most men, who prefer directness. Most men want to know up front how they can help. Jesus did too.

The Woman Who Tried to Remain Anonymous (Luke 8:40–56)

As Jesus was on his way, the crowds almost crushed him. And a woman was there who had been subject to bleeding for twelve years, but no one could heal her. She came up behind him and touched the edge of his cloak, and immediately her bleeding stopped. (Luke 8:42–44)

Imagine menstruating for twelve years! Listen to Max Lucado
describe her.

> To see her hand you need to look low. Look down. That's
> where she lives. Low to the ground. Low on the priority
> list. Low on the social scale. She's low. Can you see it? Her
> hand? Gnarled. Thin. Diseased. Dirt blackened the nails
> and stains the skin. Look carefully amid the knees and feet
> of the crowd. They're scampering after Christ. He walks.
> She crawls. People bump her, but she doesn't stop. Others
> complain. She doesn't care. The woman is desperate. Blood
> won't stay in her body. "There was a woman in the crowd
> who had had a hemorrhage for twelve years" (Mark 5:25
> NLT). Twelve years of clinics. Treatments. Herbs. Prayer
> meetings. Incantations. No health. No money. And no
> family to help. Unclean, according to the Law of Moses.
> The Law protected women from aggressive, insensitive
> men during those times of the month. In this woman's
> case severe application of the Law left her, not untouched,
> but untouchable, ceremonially unclean. The hand you see
> in the crowd? The one reaching for the robe? No one will
> touch it. Can we fault this woman's timidity? She doesn't
> know what to expect. Jesus could berate her, embarrass
> her. And the people—what will they do? What will the
> ruler of the synagogue do? He is upright. She is unclean.
> And here she is, lunging at the town guest. No wonder she
> is afraid.[3]

This woman follows Jesus through the streets. If you have traveled these cities, you know many of the streets are narrow—you can't
drive even a small car through them. The text says the crowds almost crushed Jesus. The Greek word literally means "strangled."
A celebrity and a mob. Obviously many people are making physical contact. As Jesus passes by, the bleeding woman reaches out her
hand and touches the edge of his garment.

"Who touched me?" he asked. Did Jesus know? Of course he did, but he was not going to let this woman remain anonymous. All the people denied touching him—*It wasn't me!* Peter jumped in, "Master, the people are crowding and pressing against you." *How silly. Lots of people touched you.* But Jesus was referring to a particular person and he would not continue until she identified herself. Finally she came forward and spoke up.

> Then the woman, seeing that she could not go unnoticed, came trembling and fell at his feet. In the presence of all the people, she told why she had touched him and how she had been instantly healed. Then [Jesus] said to her, "Daughter, your faith has healed you. Go in peace." (Luke 8:47–48)

Jesus called her out of the shadows and insisted she declare her faith, face her fear of exposure, and speak openly.

She reminds me of too many gifted female leaders who sit like stone. They have so much to contribute but they cannot find their voice. Some seem afraid and uncomfortable. Maybe some are simply uncertain how to participate in a gathering with brothers. Maybe some have not learned to be direct or contribute succinctly. We need to learn, because direct, honest, concise communication will foster healthy male-female working relationships.

The Woman Clawing to Be Heard (Matt. 20:20–28)

A young pastor met with me (Sue) for help. He rolled his eyes as he described Leslie, the woman who was making his life miserable. Every Sunday night, he dreaded her e-mail followed by a meeting to complain about something—the staff should be more diverse, the colors in the church were dated, the music was too loud. "I don't mind constructive criticism, and, Lord knows, we aren't perfect—but she is constantly in my face pushing her agenda—on and on and on. And the way she talks to me—as if she was my mother and I lost my homework."

He confronted her about her bulldog attitude. This just made matters worse. Now she was harassing the elders and women leaders. Everyone was sick of her calls and e-mails.

Could it be that some sisters are reluctant to speak up because they have seen the damage caused by women like Leslie?

> My advice to women is to understand that we live in a fallen society where there is inbred prejudice. My conviction is that it's going to take time, experience, and maturity to pull us out. Women, you are pioneers and you must act accordingly. You need to understand that this prejudice is still a hangover and your task is to shred it. You must proceed with caution until new patterns are established. Trust the Lord to give you your position. Men resent women when they try to force their way in. Develop a servant's heart and remember you are not competing. You are distinctive.
>
> —Dr. Howard Hendricks

Cruella in *101 Dalmatians*. The Witch in *The Lion, the Witch and the Wardrobe*. We don't want to be like these and other outspoken women characterized in literature and media! For many of us, powerful unspoken messages in our heads control our mouths like puppeteers—messages from well-intentioned mothers and Bible study teachers warning us to be quiet. How do we free ourselves? Where is the middle ground between being silent and outspoken?

We need to learn the difference between assertiveness and aggressiveness. To assert means to state or declare positively. The idea is to exhibit a direct God-confidence; what you are saying has been thought-through and is Spirit-led. The woman with the issue of blood needed to be more assertive, and there are times when we sisters need to be assertive too. We will look at an example in the next section.

However, aggression is not a productive strategy for women or men. *Aggression* comes from the Latin word for "attack." It is offensive action characterized by a militant or combative attitude. It is a chip on one's shoulder, an agenda, a pushiness. In our experience, even a hint of female aggression in a mixed-gender gathering irritates the brothers, shuts down teamwork, and is counterproductive. In stark contrast to the tongue-tied sister, this woman usually opens her mouth too much and at the wrong times. And when she does, even if it's subtle, her seething spirit spews out to pollute the environment. James and John's mother was aggressive, teaching us a good lesson from a bad example.

> Then the mother of Zebedee's sons came to Jesus with her sons and, kneeling down, asked a favor of him.
> "What is it you want?" he asked.
> She said, "Grant that one of these two sons of mine may sit at your right and the other at your left in your kingdom."
> "You don't know what you are asking," Jesus said to them. "Can you drink the cup I am going to drink?"
> "We can," they answered.
> Jesus said to them, "You will indeed drink from my cup, but to sit at my right or left is not for me to grant. These places belong to those for whom they have been prepared by my Father."
> When the ten heard about this, they were indignant with the two brothers. (Matt. 20:20–24)

What a foolish request from a foolish woman! "Mother bears" make messes. I (Sue) know. One semester, my daughter was having college housing problems. The rules barred her from being paired with the Christian roommate of her choice. I had heard horror stories of men sleeping over and I was determined that my daughter would not be exposed to such behavior. (I tell you this for sympathy, which I will need as you read on.)

I researched the system and learned that the only way the school would make exceptions to their rule was if the student had learning disabilities. My daughter had none, but I was bent on safeguarding her. For a week, I called the housing office three or four times a day—long distance—as I worked my way up the ladder to the housing director. Finally I was on the line with him—me and my aggressive, mother-bear attitude.

He asked me questions about the situation. The last question: "Does your daughter have a learning disability?" My indignant answer: "I don't label people." He interpreted my response as a "yes." I knew I had misled him, without actually lying, but I stuffed the tinge of guilt. On hanging up, I erupted with glee. I could not wait to call my daughter to tell her that I had accomplished the impossible. She was paired up with the roommate of her choice. Mother bear won.

The whole next year was a disaster. Her "Christian" roommate turned out to be a hell-raiser in disguise. There were often boys in her room, and her roommate left pregnant at the end of the semester. I spent many hours on the phone counseling my daughter on how to respond in this miserable situation, knowing that I was the cause of it all. Today, many years later, when either of us is tempted to manipulate—we look at each other, remember this fiasco, and determine to trust God. Aggression is not God's way!

John's mother wanted the best for her children too. She went to Jesus hoping to procure Jesus' favor for her sons—special privileges in his future kingdom. Those with the most power sat on the right and the left of the King. But her strategy was not the right way to approach Jesus, and it is not the way for us to approach our brothers.

We don't know if the request was her sons' idea or hers. Either way, they conspired to weasel their way to the top through a bold, aggressive request. Neither do we know why she was elected to make the request—but we do know Jesus did not appreciate her overture. Can you blame him? How obnoxious! How annoying! He responded with a rebuke. *You don't know what you are asking.* And when the other apostles learned of the incident, they were irritated too.

Notice that Jesus ignored the mother and instead addressed his response to James and John. Being ignored can add fuel to the fire and support a woman's underlying assumption that she is not valued and that she must continue to use these kinds of tactics to be heard and win her case. But she seldom does win. I have watched aggressive women burn out and be left by the wayside, fuming. In ministry, I've never seen an aggressive sister work successfully with brothers.

The Woman Who Got It Right (Mark 7:24–30)

Let's look at a woman who found that middle ground between silence and aggression. She was not afraid to tell Jesus exactly what she needed.

> Jesus left that place and went to the vicinity of Tyre. He entered a house and did not want anyone to know it; yet he could not keep his presence secret. In fact, as soon as she heard about him, a woman whose little daughter was possessed by an evil spirit came and fell at his feet. The woman was a Greek, born in Syrian Phoenicia. She begged Jesus to drive the demon out of her daughter. (Mark 7:24–26)

Jesus traveled outside Palestine and into Gentile territory to Tyre, modern-day Lebanon. He was not there to minister publicly but to secure private time to instruct his disciples.[4] But the news of his arrival leaked out, and a desperate mother found him, fell at his feet, and directly made her request. Perhaps Jesus did not appreciate the interruption.

In ministry, sisters often find they must go to their brothers for what they need. For a variety of reasons, sometimes their brothers are not receptive. Back in the nineties, I (Sue) served as the volunteer director of women's ministries in a megachurch. I was at the mercy of the male pastors for resources. But I had not yet found my voice, so during the few meetings with the senior pastor, I clammed up and did not express my needs. I taught the Bible to large groups of women—sometimes hundreds—and talked openly with my family and friends, but I was inhibited with this male minister. It's a wonder he supplied us with a budget at all.

As I interacted with this male leader, I was confused. How should I act? Forceful like a savvy businesswoman? Demure and shy like I had been taught by a Bible study leader years earlier? I did not understand that I was his spiritual sister—so I did not act like one. This Gentile woman in Mark 7 could easily have felt confused too, especially since she was not "one of his kind." But she did not let that deter her. She was direct and up front because her cause was worthy. Her daughter needed healing. My cause was worthy too. I wanted the resources to minister to thousands of women in our church. But I allowed this man to intimidate me. Not this woman! I should have taken a lesson from her. She asked directly, but her request was denied nevertheless. What do we do then?

"First let the children eat all they want," he told her, "for it is not right to take the children's bread and toss it to their dogs." (Mark 7:27)

Ouch! That hurt! Jesus painted a picture that excluded her. In the passage, the children represented his disciples who were waiting to be fed. The children's bread was figurative language for the benefits his disciples enjoyed, and the dogs were not street mongrels, but probably house pets, who sat under the table hoping for a tasty morsel to fall.[5] Jesus was not comparing her to a Gentile dog, the Jewish derogatory term for outsiders. But he still denied her request—and being compared to any dog, even a pampered pet, could not have been pleasant. But she did not allow hurt feelings to overwhelm her nor did she respond defensively. Instead, she understood that she was not on his agenda for the day. But she persisted nevertheless. She believed her need was worthy to be on his agenda.

"'Yes, Lord,' she replied, 'but even the dogs under the table eat the children's crumbs'" (Mark 7:28). Not angry but consensual words. He was right. She was not a disciple or a Jew. But she was somebody and so was her daughter. She did not want much of his time, just a crumb. And with wise, reverent words she continued her argument. He heard her out, was impressed with what he heard, and granted her request. "For such a reply, you may go; the demon has left your daughter" (v. 29). Men respect sisters who believe in their cause and are willing to make a cogent case, as long as they do so with grace and humility.

This Lebanese sister models the healthy balance between drawing back and rushing forward foolishly. What else do we need to consider as we speak with brothers?

Choose Your Battles Carefully

Brothers tell us they sometimes struggle to understand their sisters' world. As people, we have much in common—more than the things that divide us. But our perspectives and priorities on particular issues are sometimes miles apart. Brothers need a gracious, articulate sister to directly explain how over half of the human race thinks. Sometimes sisters need to persuade with gentle persistence and sometimes sisters need to hold back.

I (Sue) have worked with supportive brothers who did not always understand my perspective. For example, a man in our congregation organized an evangelistic training conference. In an effort to guarantee a large turnout, he suggested a competition between the men and women. The gender group with the most attendees would win a prize. Our women's team disliked the strategy but they determined: *If the women win, we win—and if the men win, we win too—because our men will be receiving valuable training.* Nevertheless, the women believed this competition would fall flat with females.

As the women's minister, this put me in an awkward position. As I met with the men planning the event, I walked a fine line. Was this a battle worth fighting? Where was the middle ground between acquiescing and aggression? How far should a sister push? I wanted an honest dialogue but not counterproductive wrangling. I prayed, and then consulted with my women's ministry staff. We considered the individual personalities involved and the significance of the situation, and ultimately decided not to fight this battle. Fortunately, the men later changed their minds without knowing the women's concerns.

No set rules for ministry conflict exist, and we must each prayerfully discern what is appropriate in each situation. Some situations warrant persistence, courage, and a refusal to back down. Vickie Kraft served as minister to women at a megachurch in Dallas for fourteen years. During a staff meeting, a male colleague insisted that there were no female images of God in the Bible. Vickie gave him several examples. He dismissed them and continued his argument. Vickie felt this was a battle worth fighting—a theological war she must win if the women in her church were to be valued. A third party finally helped them settle the dispute, with Vickie able to identify several maternal metaphors in Scripture that described God's character (see Isa. 49:15; Matt. 23:37).

Walk the Line

Choosing the right battles for the right reasons requires prayer, input from wise counselors, and discernment in conversing. At times, it is clear that my viewpoint will not prevail. A foolish response would be to argue, get emotional, or question a brother's judgment. The wise response is to give clear, succinct reasons or to ask for a continuance, to wait, and to continue in prayer. Many times I (Sue) have seen the Lord work on my behalf. He has orchestrated a circumstance or decision that made my argument more logical. Other times, I have backed off, waited, and learned that my approach was in error. I did not have the full picture or I was simply mistaken in my assessment. God comes through for us as we trust him!

The woman who got it right models a wise response for all sisters today. As we learn from the Bible and godly mentors—and as we pray—God will enable us to know how to effectively respond to brothers to further God's work and enhance harmony.

Sometimes women can be overreactive to men when it takes them a while to get it. The women's response can be too intense and can wind up shutting down dialogue. I want to say to them, "Just wait. You'll get your moment to communicate how that came across and you'll be a lot farther down the road if you wait." Guys can get to the point where they feel, *Am I going to have to watch everything I say because of the intense response when I screw up?* Guys have a fear. It comes from the feminist movement that says women are really here to take over. It can appear that there is no grace for the men. We all have to give some space to figure out how to do this. I want to win the war, not every battle, and the war will only be won when we are equally effective and equally unleashed for the kingdom. We say to the women, "Welcome to the staff—join the party." The reality is that we want to be effective for Christ long-term, and that does mean that some of our communication styles need to change. But if someone's hackles come up, men are not as likely to change. Then men tend to dig their heels in the sand. So women, give the guys some grace and think long-term.

—Steve Roese

Working together as sisters and brothers is sometimes complicated, but we can learn from these three women in Scripture. Somehow sisters must navigate between extremes, asking directly for what we need, applying the right strength but not too much, and resisting the temptation to be pushy or aggressive. Speak up—tell your brothers what you need or think—but with grace and wisdom.

Sisters, Stand by Your Brothers

In the gospel accounts, women disciples stood by Jesus. They were loyal and devoted—and they alone, except for John, did not desert him on the cross.

After this, Jesus traveled about from one town and village to another, proclaiming the good news of the kingdom of God. The Twelve were with him, and also some women who had been cured of evil spirits and diseases: Mary (called Magdalene) from whom seven demons had come out; Joanna the wife of Cuza, the manager of Herod's household; Susanna; and many others. These women were helping to support them out of their own means. (Luke 8:1–3)

As we observed in chapter 2, early in Jesus' ministry, a band of women began traveling with him, along with the twelve apostles. These women were never the same after their encounter with Jesus, and, like the apostles, they left everything to follow him. They were wealthy women, enjoying luxurious lifestyles back home, but they chose a nomadic life in order to serve Jesus and their brothers. These women bankrolled Jesus' ministry!

Jesus had no qualms about accepting their money. And, as we suggested in chapter 2, we don't believe they followed in silence. They were a part of his family, and, knowing Jesus, he included them when it was appropriate and he treated them well. These, and many other women, stayed with him for the long haul, despite the hardships and obstacles, and even in the midst of horror and danger.

> Many women were there [at the cross], watching from a distance. They had followed Jesus from Galilee to care for his needs. Among them were Mary Magdalene, Mary the mother of James and [Joseph], and the mother of Zebedee's sons. (Matt. 27:55–56)

What stamina and fortitude! Imagine the conversations among them as they watched their brothers turn the world upside down—then their concern as persecution escalated. They were helpless except to pray—and pray they did—especially when Jewish leaders put a contract out on Jesus' life.

Like the women who stood by Jesus, God asks sisters today to love their brothers with a godly devotion and loyalty—to pray for them, support and encourage them. But how does a sibling relationship differ from other mixed-gender relationships? Loving like a brother or sister is not the same as loving like a spouse. Both involve an emotional attachment yet they are different.

Picture a married couple facing each other, gazing into each other's eyes. This depth of intimacy is inappropriate for siblings. Instead picture a brother and sister facing forward, gazing off into the distance in the same direction. They stand side by side, focusing on a mutual goal. For sacred siblings, that goal is ministry, honoring God, and furthering his kingdom. Again, the emotional attachment of a wife versus that of a sister is different.

Knowing the difference is crucial, and siblings who are careless or foolish destroy lives and the Lord's reputation. What would Jesus applaud as appropriate for siblings? How does a sister stand by her brother?

Pursue Emotional Health

First, we must become a sister from the inside out. That means that we work hard to become emotionally healthy. We all have baggage, problems, hurts, weaknesses, faults, quirks, idiosyncrasies, and sin. We hurt because we were not loved perfectly by our parents, spouses, or friends. We lack a mother to cheer us on or a father to protect us. We have no extended family or a quirky extended family. We all share this human condition—we all live in a fallen world. The question is what have we done with our lack? Have we used it to excuse immaturity? Or have we committed to the hard work of achieving emotional health? Only emotionally healthy, siblings can work honorably together.

When we are emotionally healthy, our emotional tanks are filled by God and not people. When we are emotionally healthy, we don't need affirmation from the other gender to feel worthwhile and whole. When we are emotionally healthy, we are not nearly as vulnerable to inappropriate emotional attachments that wound our siblings and dishonor God. Sisters, our first order of business, if we want to earn a place by our brother's side, is to be ruthless in our pursuit of emotional health. Pay the price, carve out the time, do whatever is necessary to be a sister from the inside out.

Pray for Brothers and Their Families

I (Sue) minister alongside four men as full-time faculty in the Christian education department at Dallas Theological Seminary. And I have worked with brothers in the church for over fifteen years. How do I interact with them?

I don't baby, mother, or micromanage my brothers. But I pray
for them and their families. For example, one of our most-beloved
professors, Howard Hendricks, was fighting an ongoing battle with
cancer. I mentioned to him at a staff meeting that I prayed for him
regularly. He replied, "That's the best thing you could ever do for
me." It was my way of loving and supporting him as a caring sister—
and I could tell he sincerely appreciated it. Praying for our spiritual
brothers and sisters, their marriages, and their families is a wonderful way to stand by them.

Develop Relationships with Their Families

I'm intentional about developing friendships with my brothers'
wives. I ask questions about their children and attempt to get to
know them. Occasionally deep friendships between couples develop.
For example, Dr. Haddon Robinson, father of American preaching,
and Dr. Alice Mathews, who partners with Martin DeHaan in the
public radio ministry *Radio Bible Class*, are spiritual brother and sister.
They and their spouses, Bonnie and Randy, have been close friends
for many years, enjoying outings and staying in one another's homes
when traveling.

Enter Your Brothers' Worlds

Dianne Miller was community pastor and a member of the lead
pastoral team at a large Dallas church. For many years she had worked
solely with women, but as community pastor, her colleagues were
men. As a result of her new position, her reading habits changed. She
began to turn to the sports page first, knowing it was fodder for small
talk at staff meetings. Her practice was not manipulative, but a genuine effort to understand, enjoy, and enter the world of brothers.

Don't Bash Your Brothers

Eavesdrop on women's conversations and you will occasionally
hear them bash men. Some women feel oppressed by men, often with
good reason. Men have had the advantage for centuries, as Leonard
Sax points out in *Why Gender Matters*.

Many gender-based inequities persist in our society. Men remain far more likely to be CEOs of major corporations despite the fact that there is now a substantial cohort of equally well-trained women. Men are more likely to start their own businesses. Men are still more likely to be leading politicians, although women are gaining ground . . . Even when you control for occupation, education, and hours worked a significant gender gap in pay persists. Men still get paid somewhat more than women do for doing the same work, on average, both in the United States and around the world . . . Women made gains from the 1960s through the 1980s but there was no significant progress made in the United States in the gender gap between 1990 and 2000.[6]

Sometimes resentment builds because of this history, and women react with cynicism, distasteful humor, and harsh rhetoric. While understandable, this is still sin. These men are our brothers. We must defend and honor them. They aren't perfect, but neither are we. We must believe the best. Never bash a brother. In a biological family, if someone is bullying our brother, we come to his defense. If we have a beef with him, we should talk about it with him openly and respectfully. This is appropriate family behavior in the spiritual family too.

Encourage Your Brothers with Appropriate Words

> Avoid talking about really deep, personal problems with men individually.
>
> —Scott Stonehouse

When I (Sue) ministered only to women, an important part of my work was to empower these women to develop and use their gifts. Many of them were insecure and I encouraged them whenever I could. If I saw even a hint of a gift, I commented. If I saw them shine, I said so.

Years ago, teaching with one brother, I was impressed with his teaching expertise, love for students, and scholarly insight. I also noticed that he seemed unsure of himself at times. I later learned this was simply his humility, but initially I thought he needed encouragement. As was my habit from working with women, I praised him each time he taught. Several weeks into the semester, he kindly told me that my constant encouragement made him uncomfortable. He was a gentleman and did not come right out and say it with those words—but I got the message.

I realized that a relationship with a brother is different from a sister. With some women, it is almost impossible to praise them too much. Their emotional tanks are empty, and praise from a woman who represents God is like praise from God himself. It builds them up. It charges them to step out and serve God with confidence and strength. But when I praised my brother that way, it made him uncomfortable. It was not appropriate. It could easily have been misunderstood.

Now I praise my brother on special occasions, when he has won an award or excelled at a difficult task. Sometimes I express my respect for him in a public meeting, but I'm careful.

When I plan a seminary course with a male colleague, we keep the conversation focused on work. I keep e-mails friendly but to the point. Occasionally, I ask them about family, ministry, a mission trip, or something mildly personal, but not deeply intimate. I ask the Lord to show me what words are appropriate and what is over the line. I want my brothers to know that my intentions are always honorable.

My distance does not indicate a lack of sibling love but instead an abundance of discretion. I never want to be misunderstood. I want them to sense that my deepest desire is that they succeed in every way—as husbands, fathers, professors, and men of God. The best way I can help them is to pray for, encourage, support, and stand by them—but facing forward, side by side.

Support your brothers with kind words of respect and honor. But remember that the emotional connection between the two of you is different from an emotional bond with a spouse. Sisters, it is not our place to keep our brothers' emotional tanks full.

Shoulder to Shoulder

Question: What would make you uncomfortable in the workplace with a person of the opposite sex?

Response: If the person assumed that the workplace is there primarily for the establishment of caring relationships.

—Dr. Dan Allender

What characterizes healthy working relationships between brothers and sisters? We saw the way Jesus and Paul treated sisters in chapters 2 and 3. In this chapter we have examined guidelines to keep our sibling relationships healthy and holy. Sisters, speak up. Find that middle ground between silence and aggression. And stand by your brothers—but remember that a sibling relationship is different from a spouse. Your place is not to fill their emotional tanks. Work hard side by side, facing forward and focused on a mutual goal. When we learn to stand shoulder to shoulder, ministry will change for the better. God's work will explode because the whole team is on board, loving each other as a family should.

DISCUSSION QUESTIONS

1. Have you ever observed women clamming up in a mixed-gender setting? If so, why do you think this occurs?

2. (For women only) Do you tend to speak up less in a mixed-gender group? If so, can you identify why? Explain.

3. What is the difference between assertiveness and aggressiveness? How do you respond to women who exhibit these qualities? How do you respond when men exhibit these same qualities?

4. How should a godly woman speak and act in a mixed-gender group?

5. Do you have experience working with the opposite sex on a ministry team? If so, what have you learned that could help others who want to live out sibling love?

6. How can a Christian woman pursue emotional health?

7. Respond to the suggestions in the chapter designed to help women work effectively with brothers. Any disagreements? Any ideas you would echo?

Chapter 8

For Brothers' Eyes Only

Rise up, O men of God!
The church for you doth wait,
Her strength unequal to her task;
Rise up, and make her great!

—WILLIAM P. MERRILL

(OKAY WOMEN, LET'S BE FAIR . . . *the guys read your chapter, so go ahead and glean from theirs too.*)

The term "glass ceiling" was coined in the early 1980s to refer to the reality that men held the top-level corporate positions. It was a "ceiling" because women were limited in how far they could advance. The term "glass" was used because the limitations were not always obvious. Today's reality is that men and women work together as peers in corporate America. The glass ceiling is shattering in government and business. Today we have female CEOs, Supreme Court Justices, and U.S. Senators.

While the workplace offers greater opportunities for women, there is still room for improvement, and for women this can be discouraging. Charlotte Whitton captured the thoughts of many women in business when she said, "Whatever women do they must do twice as well as men to be thought half as good."[1] While I (Henry) don't completely agree with her view, I understand the frustration in her words.

Seeing the Benefits of Women in Ministry

Men, the church has to be a different environment where we value the God-given gifts and skills of both men and women as we serve together as colaborers in Christ. Experience shows us that women do serve together with men, sometimes in leadership, sometimes as volunteers. The purpose of this chapter is not to argue what roles are open to women. We can all agree that the Bible encourages women to minister to other women. Certain positions in today's churches are not mentioned in the Bible, and each church invites women to serve in different ways, as the leadership directs. So in this chapter, I will coach men not on *where* we can serve together, but *how* we can serve together with women as siblings—as brothers and sisters in the body of Christ.

At first glance you may have some reservations or concerns. We have all heard stories of men who failed when they worked in ministry with women. Of course there are challenges, but there are also valid reasons why we need to see the value of such an opportunity. Let me offer a few reasons that will shed some light on the wonderful benefits of men partnering with women in ministry.

> There must be a conscious decision to step back and say, "Are women valuable? Do they bring anything to the table? Do they bring something to the table in other organizations, and if so, can they bring something to this organization?" A lot of men genuinely don't believe women have something to bring to the table. And when women bring it in a different way, it says to them, "See, they don't." And women do have a tendency to lead somewhat differently. That's a general statement but women sometimes communicate differently, and when we are used to our own style, that can come across as too much caring, too

> much emotion, or too much collaboration—whereas the woman may be a dynamic leader but she doesn't lead like us. And we must understand that it's valuable. Many pastors are invested or vested in organizations led by women, maybe their 401K or stock in corporations, but it never occurs to them that a woman can bring something to the table in the church. Part of that is just tradition.
>
> —Steve Roese

Women Bring a Unique Perspective

When men and women work together, much can be accomplished. The good news is that each of us brings a unique perspective! A generation ago philosopher and writer George Santayana wrote, "Friends are generally of the same sex, for when men and women agree, it is only in the conclusions; their reasons are always different."[2]

I laughed when I read Santayana's words, but there is an element of truth to what he writes. Men and women think differently! By valuing the differences, however, we have the opportunity to accomplish so much more. I love what Dr. Michael Lawson from Dallas Theological Seminary said in an interview:

We make better ministry decisions when we have more women on staff. Just as a husband is a fool who does not listen to his wife, men in ministry are fools if they do not listen to women. I learned to listen to my wife and we make far better decisions together. The same principle is true in leading a church. Godly women bring balance and a unique perspective to our decisions. For many years in our staff meetings, we men would meet together and make decisions. Then we would go home and tell our wives what we had decided. She would say, "Have you thought about this? Did you consider that?" She would ask some penetrating questions that we had not considered. Then in our next meeting, we men would bring up these issues and "change our minds." It was inefficient. Today godly women on staff make men aware of issues they would never have considered. The whole church benefits.[3]

Women Effectively Minister to Women

Who better to minister to women than women? We've already seen this in the ministry of the New Testament church. It's true in your congregation as well. More than half of your congregation is female. You have women in the pews and future women in the nursery, and one thing they all have in common is that they need attention (as do the men). Of women ministering to women, Howard Hendricks says,

> I think this is one of the missing ingredients in ministry today. I think a woman has an incredible ministry because she is a woman. A woman can minister in areas where I have no background—a man knows zero in terms of female experience. Bringing (my wife) Jeanne into my counseling ministry revolutionized it. She would get after me because I was being too hard and the woman always knew she had someone on her team.[4]

Can you imagine the "success" of a women's ministry with a guy in charge? I smile when I see how men and women of my church prepare for retreats. In addition to content, women concern themselves with details that never register on our radar. They plan for decorations and games that will bring women together into intimate relationships. Men, on the other hand, are concerned about who is bringing the chips and salsa. Whatever game we play has to include a ball and the need for pain relief cream afterward.

Women Are Gifted in Many Ways

I have tremendous respect for my pastor as a theologian and teacher. Each Sunday I sit on the edge of my seat, excited about the message that God has put on his heart. One of the things I appreciate about him is that he loves wrestling with Scripture. He won't avoid tough passages. He attacks them head-on with a desire to fully understand the author's intent.

When he finds himself with more questions than answers, he calls people he respects to help him with his thought process. Everyone in our church knows his favorite person to call. This individual is a valuable resource who has helped him on many occasions accurately interpret a tough passage. His favorite resource is both an author and a seminary graduate. Her name is Sandi. Yup, his favorite resource is a woman. She is as smart as a whip and she has been encouraged from the pulpit many times when my pastor publicly expresses his appreciation for her help.

Women are indeed gifted in a variety of ways. In many churches, women's Bible studies have tremendous participation from women. Sure, they love the fellowship, but women also love great teaching, which is a gift that many of them are able to bring to a church body by way of leading small groups, children's ministries, and youth groups. It is vitally important for the church today to be training women to become strong teachers.

Women Care About People

I once taught a Sunday school class and used a sad illustration where someone in the story was horribly embarrassed. The eyes of two teen girls welled up with tears. Why? It was just a story, but they cared for the character who was embarrassed. None of the guys had any kind of emotional response.

Sure, men care about people too, but showing care is more acceptable for women than it is for men. We must encourage and empower women *and* men to use these needed gifts of care and compassion to touch the lives of others.

If you need evidence of practical, women-initiated care, watch what happens in your church when a health issue strikes a family. Who organizes the meals to be brought over to the house? It's the women. When I had surgery two years ago, I was visited by men and women. The men came into my hospital room and made jokes about my scar, but it was the women who brought me something to read and snacks to eat. When I got home, I was visited by my friend and coworker, Jill Scott, who had organized a collection to buy gift cards for restaurants for me and my family. She collected more than five hundred dollars in gift cards! Why did she do this? Simple. She cared for me, and her thoughtful caring turned into action that had a lasting (and tasty) impact.

Men Who Are Not Convinced . . .

Unfortunately, we have men in ministry who find women a distraction or a danger. Is it possible that some men believe that the threat of temptation outweighs the benefits of working together?

Lawson argues that these men "blame women for what is going on in their own heads. To them I say, 'This is your problem!' It's a man's job to maintain healthy boundaries. You are in charge of your mind. In Galatians 5:23 we see that the Spirit gives us self-control."[5]

It's a sad reality that there are men in ministry who avoid working with women because of the potential dangers. We will discuss in a later chapter how healthy boundaries can limit these potential dangers. Emotionally healthy men *can* work side by side with women and honor God as they do so. The question is, How do we convince the skeptics and bring out the best in everyone? When you think of women in ministry, do you see the problems or the potential?

> I was speaking at a church where the men thought they were being so progressive. They hired a woman on staff and decided that she could come to their staff meetings with the condition that she kept her mouth shut!
> —Dr. Howard Hendricks

Tips for Working Together

Would my earlier quote from Charlotte Whitton of women having to "work twice as hard as men to be thought half as good" be true in the church today? I sure hope not. How can men best work together with women in ways that are effective and inclusive?

Understand That Women Feel a Difference

One of my heroes in business was a woman named Violet. Her company hired her in 1986 to head the human resources department. She was the first female to occupy a position in the company above manager level.

She confided in me that when she first started at her company, she would do all her typing after hours with her door shut. Why? She wanted to make sure the men saw her as a leader and not as a secretary. Please understand . . . she had great respect for secretaries, but she was a leader in the organization. She felt the men would view her differently if they saw her typing away at her desk. That concern would never enter the mind of a man, but it did a woman because she could feel a difference.

Men need to recognize that women are very aware when they are being treated differently, which is why it is important for men to be inclusive. At this point you may be scratching your head, wondering, "What difference?" For some men it may be difficult to define the real difference that women feel. Let me provide you a few examples to consider.

At an annual leaders' retreat, Cindy was not asked to present her work history and experience as was custom for new members of the leadership team. Male leaders were given the opportunity, but Cindy was excluded. Was it deliberate? Was it an oversight? We don't know, but Cindy felt the difference.

Julie is a female associate professor, an award-wining teacher who is popular with students. With more than fifteen years of experience, she has not been promoted to full professorship while her younger, less qualified male colleagues have been. Was the omission deliberate? Was it an oversight? We don't know, but Julie felt the difference.

I have a good friend named Sharon who serves as a vice president in her company. After serving in that role for a few years, a man was hired to head up another department. At a staff meeting several weeks later, the new vice president thanked the team of leaders for taking him to lunch and meeting with him to help him better understand the company. When Sharon came on board, she did not get that kind of welcome. It would have been easy for two or more of the vice presidents to take her to lunch to welcome her when she started. Was her exclusion deliberate? Was it an oversight? We don't know, but Sharon felt the difference.

All three of these instances were missed opportunities to value women in their respective roles. Instead of affirming them and building them up, the women were soured by the experience because they could feel "the difference."

Drop Demeaning Language

The spoken word is powerful. In the workplace and in ministry, professional language is an expectation, but unfortunately, it is not always the reality. Even in the twenty-first-century, a woman is sometimes called "honey," "sugar," "dear," and "sweetie" by someone other than her mother or husband. Even worse than the words used, however, is when a woman is spoken to in a patronizing manner. This can only lead to animosity and tension that will be counterproductive. No one likes to be patronized, and women are no exception. They want to be respected and valued.

> Even as gracious as our team is and as wonderful as we get along, I think the sexual joke overtones still exist, and it's very male. I don't think we as men really realize how damaging and uncomfortable that is for the women. It's not foul but you can sense "let's not go any further." I don't think we would do that at the dinner table with our wives and daughters. It would never happen there. But we will do it with women we work with. And at the table if we did it, the mom would slap us all down, but the female coworker doesn't necessarily have that authority.
>
> —Steve Roese

The key is to monitor your own speech to make sure it is professional. Be on guard for commonly used phrases that men should avoid. If you are surprised or caught off guard, I would not suggest telling a female coworker that you "got caught with your pants down." There is certainly a better way to communicate what happened.

If you struggle with unprofessional speech, it is a great idea to ask your Christian sister for help. Simply say, "If I ever come across as demeaning in my speech, would you please bring it to my attention?" One thing I know about women . . . they love to help.

Using professional speech does not mean that the workplace can't be enjoyable, but it guarantees that it can be a place where both men and women feel valued.

Value Sisters' Contributions

"There are many advantages of men and women partnering—a wider understanding of people, perspectives, and situations," said Howard Hendricks. "I find a woman brings to a committee what in most cases 90 percent of men would not even think of. The change will almost always be for the better, but her voice must be respected. Adding more women will change ministry radically and positively. It will give us balance."[6] Bill Hybels also sees the value of a woman's contribution in ministry:

> You learn something about life by being a mom that you don't by being a dad. You learn something about the church by growing up in it as a little girl, that's different than you do growing up in it as a little boy. And I think there's richness in the kind of cross pollination of ideas sharing that happens when you get perspective from both genders and you see the church family from both genders and you see the future of what the church ought to be like from both gender perspectives. I just think it is a better way to provide quality leadership for the church.[7]

Several years ago I organized a luncheon at work for seminary students. A date was set in advance and I ordered a boxed lunch that I thought they would enjoy. When the students arrived, they helped me set up the tables before we began. After eating I gave a short devotional and thanked the students for their service in the company. The lunch went well, but something seemed to be missing. The next year I decided to turn the luncheon over to one of the women on my staff. Landra made an immediate change by inviting the seminary students' spouses. On the day of the lunch, I walked into a decorated room with tables already set up. We had music and an awesome buffet. I still gave a devotional and thanked them for their service, but this year the luncheon was a huge success. Before the students left, each one was given a gift . . . and their wives got one too. Landra brought tremendous value to the event and the seminary students were greatly encouraged. Care to guess who organized the event the next year?

Work with the Differences

It is not earth-shattering news to discover that men and women are different. Guys have known that since kindergarten. We talked about this fact already in chapter 5. We are different in the way we look, think, and feel. Women generally talk more and cry more . . . and they see things differently. So why can't we work with the differences to make us stronger?

I don't like the common artificial distinction that women are more emotive than men. But I do think women bring a different sensitivity to interactions with men, and this is helpful and productive. I work with a good number of women in leadership roles in my organization and I find them to be professional, creative, hardworking, and dedicated. But they also bring something else to the job. More so than the males, they remind me of the spiritual dimension behind the day-to-day issues of running an organization. The women with whom I work constantly pray for me and encourage me to pray more. I can honestly say that I do a better job as a seminary president because I work with these Christian women leaders.

—Dr. Frank James

Recognize and take advantage of the differences! I work with two women and I will often seek out their counsel on relational issues where I know they will offer a different view. In my role as chaplain, I work with a committee of six that discusses issues for benevolent giving. Of the six, half are women and they have been an invaluable resource.

Invite Sisters into the Conversation

Imagine being in a church staff meeting consisting of seven men and one woman. The guys don't see a problem, but remember that women can feel a difference. Some women may be more inclined to listen in an effort to avoid appearing pushy or aggressive. Women know that men don't care for pushy women . . . so they listen.

What can you do to invite them into the conversation? Simple! Say something like, "Karen, I'd love to know your thoughts on this issue." When you thank her for the feedback, she will already be more inclined to present her views in the future. The other men will see the value you place in her opinion and they will begin to value it too.

> Once you have women on staff and that corner has been turned, it's almost ironic, because even though there are different styles, in my experience we have to play to that less and less rather than more. We are all equal here and I find the women mix it up with the guys—going toe-to-toe with the men—it's almost the ultimate compliment to have an environment where you don't have men on eggshells, thinking, "I need to tone down," or worrying about pulling back, or women thinking, "I need to be aggressive." We can be together and be who we are and it's fun.
>
> Steve implemented the red flag plan, a stroke of genius. We heard from strong personalities, both male and female, that the quieter ones were getting run over in our meetings. So Steve brought out these NFL red flags and put them all around the table. And in the middle of any

> debate or discussion, if someone felt like someone else was over the top or getting too aggressive, you could throw the flag. It was serious but it was also fun because it brought everyone back.
>
> —Dr. Andy McQuitty

Speak Up for Sisters

How do you feel about women working with men as sisters in ministry? I hope by now you see a value in it. If so, speak up! As we saw earlier, Howard Hendricks has been speaking up for sisters for many years. You can too as they serve in their God-given roles.

When you get into discussions with men who see problems and not possibilities in working with women, it's time to speak up! When you hear guys using humor in poor taste around women, don't wait for her to say something, only to appear prudish. Speak up! As Barnabas spoke up for Paul when the other leaders saw problems, we can speak up for women because we know the possibilities.

Steve Roese advises that men create space for a woman to succeed. "People tend to gravitate toward people who can get it done," he says. "Once a woman has succeeded, then nobody cares [about gender issues], in general. Cross that hurdle and it makes a big difference."[8]

Brothers and Sisters

This is not an issue that we can avoid addressing any longer. John Ortberg writes,

A working relationship between spiritual brothers and sisters is not formal like the military. It's not bottom line like business. It's not emotionally intimate like marriage. It's about family and friendship. But family and friendship is messy. Add gender to the mix and ministry relationships become even more complex. We need to consider how to become wise and skilled at mixed-gender relationships—and it will take work—but we believe the benefits are worth the effort.[9]

We live in an age where women serve in significant roles in business and government, and yet in the church, women have very few opportunities. Of course, I'm not advocating cultural conformity, but as we look at the glass ceiling in the church, how much of it is based on Scripture and how much of it is tradition or personal preference?

I have a friend named Jennifer who is gifted financially and uses her gifts to manage the finances at her church, and yet she is not included on the leadership committee. The committee includes pastors, elders, deacons, and leaders of various church ministries. All of the representatives on this committee are male. When the pastor was asked why Jennifer was not on the committee, he replied, "What will we do on deer hunts?" Was her exclusion from this leadership committee based on the words of the apostle Paul? No, the pastor just didn't want a woman on the annual deer hunt.

Brothers, it is time for us to open our eyes and see not only the gifts that women have been given, but the value of women who utilize those gifts. Can you imagine what God will do when we *all* use the amazing gifts he has given us?

DISCUSSION QUESTIONS

1. Have you witnessed the "glass ceiling" in your workplace? If so, describe its impact.

2. Do you agree with Dr. Lawson that better ministry decisions result when women are consulted? Why or why not?

3. What examples can you offer that support the premise, "Women care about people!" Do you believe women care more about people than men do? Discuss the relationship between compassion and gender.

4. Can you give examples of supportive language or demeaning language in a mixed-gender setting?

5. John Ortberg insists that mixed-gender friendships are messy. Can you give some examples? He also says they are "worth the work." What are some benefits for men, women, the church, and God's reputation?

Part 2

SAFEGUARDS FOR
SIBLINGS

Chapter 9

The Elephant in the Family Room

You don't choose your family. They are God's gift to you,
and you are to them.

—ARCHBISHOP DESMOND TUTU

SAMANTHA STEPPED INTO THE elevator and greeted the male seminary student already standing there. "Hi."

"I can't talk to you. I'm married."

The silence was shocking as they completed their short trip to the third floor. Weeks later, Samantha confessed to a friend her continued bewilderment and pained confusion. "I was not flirting. I did not want to woo him away from his wife. I had no romantic interest in him at all. I was simply being polite."

What caused such an extreme reaction to a sister's platonic greeting? Why did he refuse to even say "hello"?

We don't think it was because of his conviction that men and women are different or because of his view of what the Bible teaches about women's roles. Instead, we wonder if he saw this woman as a threat to his purity and his marriage—more of a temptress than a sister. Could this be the hidden motivation and possibly the root cause that divides some Christian brothers and sisters today? We believe sexual temptation is the elephant in the family room that everyone knows is there, but nobody talks about. Some men and women will not admit this reality even to themselves. This fear of sexual temptation is personal, uncomfortable, and possibly even shameful, yet it is powerful and colors our responses to one another. To protect oneself from sexual temptation is wise. It's critical that we do because we all remember too many instances when a gifted pastor left town with a single woman he was counseling, destroying his family and ministry. We hear stories of a wife and mother abandoning her family and running away with the choir director. These moral failures tarnish God's reputation and blacken his name.

We want to explore this issue of sexual temptation, the taboo subject for many Christians. We are exploring a secret world, where only the Lord and individuals are privy, and sometimes the individual isn't even in touch with his or her true motives and fears.

A Call to Holiness

Before we criticize the young man in the elevator, we should applaud him for his desire to protect himself and his marriage. He takes Paul's words seriously in 1 Thessalonians 4:2–8:

> For you know what commands we gave you through the Lord Jesus. For this is God's will: that you become holy, that you keep away from sexual immorality, that each of you know how to possess his own body in holiness and honor, not in lustful passion like the Gentiles who do not know God. In this matter no one should violate the rights of his brother or take advantage of him, because the Lord is the avenger in all these cases, as we also told you earlier and warned you solemnly. For God did not call us to impurity but in holiness. Consequently the one who rejects this is not rejecting human authority but God, who gives his Holy Spirit to you. (NET)

God did not call us to impurity but to holiness! This young man was attempting to "keep away from sexual immorality" and to "possess his own body in holiness and honor, not in lustful passion like [those] who don't know God." Good for him. We understand his fears but question his strategy. His approach is to cut himself off from contact with most women. He has decided not to look at them or talk to them. He thinks if he secludes himself from women, he is safe.

In the world of ministry, sexual indiscretion is the sin above all sins. It is the sin that says "pack up your desk right now." It is the sin that can turn you into a divorcee or a weekend parent. It soils your reputation and blackballs your future. Your years of preparation and your degrees, honors, books, and whatever else you have labored so hard to build could be washed away in an instant.

Living in an oversexed society makes it difficult to work together as brothers and sisters. The culture attempts to program us to view one another as sexual objects instead of persons. Some Christians see through the lies. Other believers struggle every day. For many it comes and goes. Sometimes we have victory for a season and then we fall back into unexpected temptation. We are committed to sexual purity and suddenly we find ourselves attracted to someone inappropriate. We don't know why we feel like this, but we know we must strategize a plan that is honorable and act on it. This plan must be fair to the person we strangely find appealing. They are often unaware, and we want to treat them kindly. At the same time, we must be ruthless in protecting our purity and our covenants. This is true for both men and women, although the battle often surfaces in different ways for each gender.

Segregation Is Not the Answer

Jesus called his followers to holiness, but Jesus would not have turned his back on the woman in the elevator. All-out segregation is not the answer. The man on the elevator displayed a separatist attitude, and when that kind of attitude is unexamined and extreme, the end result is disastrous for God's mission on earth, causing the marginalization and neglect of over half the human race. You see,

Samantha is also a seminary student. She too has heard the call of God. She too hopes to serve God out of her gifts. But whether or not doors open for Samantha sometimes depends on men like the one she encountered in the elevator. If he perceives her as a temptress instead of a sister, she isn't likely to find herself serving on his team.

Where did this young man, a future pastor, learn to treat women this way? How will this attitude play out when he is entrusted with a church comprised of 60 percent women?[1] How likely is he to hire a woman on his staff? How likely is he to consider the opinions of women as he makes decisions that determine the direction of his ministry, again comprised of more women than men?

I find this concern about sexual temptation often overstressed and used as an excuse to marginalize women. I believe men and women can and should work together and I believe they can do this effectively without inappropriate attractions.

The first question when working with a woman is not "how do I protect myself?" but "how can I encourage her gifts for the kingdom?" My first assumption is not about the potential for danger, but about the potential for greater ministry.

I do worry a bit that behind the fear of temptation is a false view of female sexuality. For centuries, the church viewed women as bewitching seductresses. I believe this is a false perspective that fails to appreciate the life-transforming work of Christ in the lives of men and women.

I do acknowledge that inappropriate feelings can occur between men and women working together—just as inappropriate feelings can occur between men and men, and women and women. But I am not convinced that the *possibility* of sin should inhibit Christians from working together. If this line of logic is followed, no Christian would work with any other Christian.

—Dr. Frank James

His approach is echoed through the pages of the writings of many of the early church fathers. Remember Tertullian's scathing indictments against women? She is "the gateway of the Devil . . . the unsealer of the forbidden tree . . . the first rebel against divine law."[2] Because of women the death of Jesus was necessary.[3] Before Origen would work with women, he castrated himself.[4] Would Augustine or Origen have spoken to the young woman on the elevator?

Is their approach biblical? Is it wise? Does it work? Has it protected male leaders from indiscretions and immorality? And does it ultimately further God's kingdom work here on earth—or does it actually hinder it? No matter how well meaning this young man was, we assert that his attitudes and methods are *not* biblical. This is *not* the way Jesus saw and treated women.

And this approach has *not* protected marriages and kept leaders from dishonoring God. This is the way of the Pharisees and the way of the Taliban,[5] and in the end, this approach has done great harm to God's mission. But if separation is not the answer, what is? How do we navigate these tensions—especially sexual tensions?

> Of course, there is a need for caution. I think temptation will always be present, but what is the appropriate response? To walk around with your eyes closed? To refuse to work with attractive women? And what is a woman supposed to do? Refuse to work with men in an attempt to avoid being a temptation? Should men and women refuse to work together in order to avoid the possibility of inappropriate emotional bonds being created? No. I think those are all silly and extreme. I think this is an area where there simply must be a personal struggle for holiness. Obviously this involves being cautious and having certain boundaries, but with those safeguards in place to help prevent sin, then I think men and women can work together productively and joyfully.
>
> —Scott Stonehouse

That's what we will discuss in the following chapters. What will enable us to minister together, while guarding our integrity and the Lord's good name? First we will examine Jesus' attitude toward promiscuous women. He was merciful to those who fell into sexual sin, even though he challenged them to leave their sin and walk in holiness. We never want to be soft on sin, but some Christians are so harsh and judgmental toward others, and toward themselves, that it hinders their ability to take positive protective steps. We need to accept that we will at times be tempted, and, instead of running in shame, we need to learn how to handle those thoughts and feelings. We need to learn how to stop our prudish denials and instead ask for help, keeping one another accountable. We will suggest some new strategies for churches and ministries to help their struggling workers conquer temptation, without segregation.

Second, we must explore what fences we can put in place to protect ourselves and others from temptation in a sibling relationship. There are some wise universal boundaries—but, at the same time, the fences may look different for different people and in different situations. For example, there are some people to whom we find ourselves more sexually attracted than others. What do we do? Is it possible to set up stronger fences and still minister with them—or should we run? These are heavy issues and thorny situations. They impact people's lives, our work for the Lord, and his reputation. We need to be proactive and have plans in hand.

It is also important that we tackle the topic of pornography and its impact on those involved. We will argue that this practice greatly distorts how men and women view the opposite sex. This epidemic is taking its toll on the church today—often in unseen ways. Damaged sibling relationships in the faith family are another tragic repercussion—and we will explore why.

How can we look and act like safe siblings in an oversexed culture? That is another important topic—our dress, demeanor, style, bearing, mannerisms, courtesies, and conduct. Men and women are sometimes unaware when they are being a stumbling block for a brother or sister. It's challenging when the latest fashion designers seem to compete for who can be the most brash and provocative. How can men and women be stylish *and* safe? We want to tackle this topic, not as a list of rules, but as relating to a heart attitude. We think honorable appearance and actions will follow.

Finally, we want to consider how sibling relationships impact spouses. A newlywed male seminary student raised this issue in class. "My wife is uncomfortable with my working with other women. What can I do?" How should siblings communicate to their spouses as they work with someone of the opposite sex? How can they *both* understand that this is good for everyone? What promotes jealousy? How is it squelched? How can we work with our spouses to ensure that the sibling relationship is safe?

Our goal as we wrestle with these issues is to protect—but not to segregate—sisters and brothers as they work together in ministry. Let's talk about the elephant in the family room—honestly—in order to promote healthy relationships in the faith family that glorify God and strengthen his church.

DISCUSSION QUESTIONS

1. Consider the encounter in the elevator. Why do you think this future pastor reacted this way? In your opinion, how prevalent is his attitude?

2. Have you ever experienced the fallout from a pastor's sexual indiscretions? (No names, please.) If so, describe them in general to the group.

3. Why is it important that Christians deal seriously with sexual temptation?

Chapter 10

New Lighting in the Church

Like men with sore eyes: they find the light painful, while the darkness,
which permits them to see nothing, is restful and agreeable.
—DIO CHRYSOSTOM

JONATHAN SAFRAN FOER, a Jewish New Yorker in his twenties, collected memories of his family—photos, cards, false teeth, handfuls of dirt—all sealed in individual plastic bags and mounted on a wall. Eager to know more about his family roots after the death of his grandparents, Jonathan embarks on an elusive quest to Ukraine, specifically to explore what happened to them during World War II.

Through a series of mishaps and adventures, he locates a relative in the Ukrainian countryside. Now elderly, she lives alone in a tiny house barely visible, surrounded by fields of sunflowers nearly as tall as the house. She asks Jonathan, "Tell me, is the war over then?" For nearly sixty years she's been hiding in that sunflower field.[1]

Hiding can be harmful. Think of an oozing wound on your arm. Instead of inspecting it carefully, treating it with antibiotic, and leaving it exposed to the air to heal, you simply slap a Sesame Street Band-Aid on it and go your way. My (Sue's) husband tells the story of his great-grandmother's unnecessary death. While she was shelling green beans, a piece lodged deep in her fingernail bed. Busy and distracted, she ignored the injury. Soon infection festered but she continued to disregard red streaks and swelling. Ultimately toxicity spread and killed her. Hiding sin kills too.

Many churches create an ethos conducive to hiding sin,[2] a practice we believe ultimately makes the church vulnerable to *more—not less—sin*, especially sexual sin. It has become the sin above all sins—horrible, abominable, appalling, beastly, detestable, heinous, shameful—and unspeakable, the one sin that we hide at all costs, the one sin we don't share with our spouse or best friend. It is *the* taboo subject. We don't teach or preach about it. Leaders don't admit they struggle—and what stays in the dark has a secret place to grow, the perfect incubator.

When we hear about couples who leave the church to divorce without ever asking for help, we wonder why. Yet, we know how easy it is to hide behind a mask of spirituality. Will people at church accept, understand, and aid us when we confess our sin to one another—especially if we are leaders? We are embarrassed, afraid, proud.

Often, our willingness to confess depends on the sin. Sins on the "approved list" are easy to tell—selfishness, pride, anger, even general lust—but it's dangerous to confess sins on the blacklist. Specific sexual sins rank high there: habitually savoring a forbidden sexual fantasy in your mind, deliberately pursuing a risky relationship with a married member of your small group or work, surfing for pornography hits in the middle of the night. Listen to the words of a pastor who hid his sexual addiction for ten years, all the while carrying on his day-to-day responsibilities in his church and speaking all over the country.

> I wish we in the church did a better job conveying God's love for sinners. From the church, I felt mainly judgment. I cannot bring my sin to the church until it has been neatly resolved into a warm, uplifting testimony. For example, if I had come to the church in the midst of my addiction to

lust, I would have been harshly judged. That, in fact, is why I had to write my article anonymously. Even after the complete cycle of confession and forgiveness, people still wrote in comments, "The author cannot possibly be considered a Christian." . . . We in the church could learn from Alcoholics Anonymous. Somehow they require accountability and communicate the Immanuelness of God. He is with you when you succeed and when you fail. He does not wait with folded arms for you to pick yourself up out of the gutter. His hands are stretched out toward you, eager to help. Where are the hands of the church?[3]

Jesus' hands are eager to embrace sinners bound in sexual sin, as we will observe in detail in the next chapter. Jesus loved sinners with sibling love. He had mercy on them. He did not condone their sinful acts or attitudes. He did not wash away the consequences of their sin. He demanded they change. But he did so in a way that was respectful and not demeaning. He loved them like a sibling and helped them to see themselves that way. His magnetic love compelled them, calling them into the light.

Create an Ethos to Expose Blacklist Sins

Light heals. A jaundiced baby needs to be exposed to intense bright light to become healthy. Sunshine feeds God's green earth through photosynthesis. Secrecy is counterproductive. Often the first step into the light is telling a trusted friend or counselor.

Confess your sins to one another and pray for one another so that you may be healed. The prayer of a righteous person has great effectiveness. . . . My brothers and sisters, if anyone among you wanders from the truth and someone turns him back, he should know that the one who turns a sinner back from his wandering path will save that person's soul from death and cover a multitude of sins. (James 5:16, 19–20 NET)

When we are struggling, the Bible exhorts us to come out of hiding and into Jesus' arms. The twin doctrines of compassion and confession work together as powerful medicines. But we grieve to say that, in our experience, neither is practiced in many churches today, at least not related to sins on the blacklist. We need places that welcome our confession, no matter its nature.

Strategies for Siblings

Consider strategies to light up your ethos. Provide safe caregivers willing to go the distance with messy people. Designate someone on staff as the "go-to" guy and gal. Set up accountability groups. Leaders, admit your imperfections and vulnerabilities. *Talk about it!*

Recently, in Lesa's church, the pastor addressed the issue of pornography in a powerful sermon. Listen to this insightful comment he made about bringing blacklist sins into the light.

> Black-list confessions are messy, requiring skilled caregivers, Jesus with skin on. Confessing may be harder than anything. You don't want to confess to just anyone. Choose wisely whom you share your deepest secrets with; choose someone who cares enough about your relationship with God to get angry with your sin. Who is your confessor? Your confessor is your doctor, not your cheerleader. When I go to the doctor, I don't want him to see something that is killing me and say, "Oh, that's bad. But hang in there because I believe in you!" You need a doctor who says, "Let's set up a plan to treat this right now. We can't wait."[4]

In the seminary where Sue teaches, a student confessed his addiction to pornography in a chapel message aimed at funneling struggling students to secure help.[5] Praise God—but we need more.

Like the Ukrainian woman hiding in the sunflowers, people decay in the darkness of sexual sin. We look forward to the day when repentant pornographers and prostitutes are drawn to churches the way wild women flocked to the arms of Jesus. In that day, people in the streets will be astounded at the power of God's love. Families once torn apart by sexual sin will be healed, and sisters and brothers will partner together in an ethos of health and harmony.

DISCUSSION QUESTIONS

1. Have you ever been part of a ministry where people were open about sexual temptation? If so, how was this ethos created?
2. What do you think would result if people could be more open about their struggles with sexual temptation?
3. Why do you think so few ministries provide an open ethos to talk about this?
4. Specifically, how might Christians develop healthy ways to help one another with lust and sexual temptation?
5. Who is your "go-to" person, the one who knows you well, and whom you trust to ask you the personal, tough questions that will help you in matters of purity?

Chapter 11

Jesus and Wild Women

Dear God, My brother told me about being born
but it doesn't sound right.

—MARSHA

I (SUE) STIRRED THE EGGS ON my plate and made polite conversation with a half-dozen women circled around the breakfast table. I was the retreat speaker and this was an opportunity to learn more about the women attending. Next to me sat Briana, a tall black woman with sculptured features, saucer eyes, and a thick British accent. While the other women laughed and shared stories of late night games and conversations, Briana's downcast eyes seldom left her plate. I wondered why, so I softly attempted to engage her.

"Where are you from, Briana?"

"Haiti—my family lives in Haiti."

"What brings you to Dallas?" I inquired.

Her answers were evasive at first, but as she sensed my sincere desire to know her story, the words gushed out. Barbara, the woman sitting next to her, placed her hand on the woman's arm. Briana spoke of her escape from poverty in Haiti, deception once she arrived, and several years in "the life," as she called it. She had been off the streets for almost a year, thanks to Barbara, who dedicated her days and resources to giving women like Briana a roof over their heads, job training, mentoring, and, most importantly, new life with Jesus.

I was humbled and awed by Barbara's courage and her fierce determination to fight for women caught in "the life." And I was glad she and Briana had come. It took guts to join "squeaky clean" white women at a Bible church retreat. None of us is squeaky clean, of course, but few women attending were in the habit of sharing breakfast with hookers either. I hugged Briana, thanked her for sharing her story, and prayed for her.

If you had asked me the day before if I wanted to eat breakfast with an ex-hooker, I'm not sure what my answer might have been. I remember when I ministered in prisons that sometimes when I held inmates' hands to pray, I fought against feeling dirty. But more and more I realize these women are just like me. Jesus is helping me love them wholeheartedly, and, strangely, in the process also helping me to accept myself, flaws and all.

That morning, I walked away from Briana and Barbara, honored to be a servant of Jesus, who alone can transform Brianas with his amazing love. And I praised God for her mentor, sitting quietly next to her, doing the work of the gospel. I might have been teaching the Bible that weekend, but Barbara was living the Bible. The last shall be first.

Sensual Images and Messages

We are surrounded by promiscuity. The media hypes sex. Families waiting to pay for groceries must trudge through a gauntlet of magazine covers flaunting peeking breasts, jeweled belly buttons, and headlines full of bedroom instructions. But who needs pictures? The teens in line ahead of you may flash nude midriffs and cleavage—just in everyday school clothes. What do you think as you see them? Our first reaction is irritation and disgust. What is it with kids today? Why are they calling attention to themselves? They have to know what kinds of thoughts they are planting in other people's minds! These are all normal responses to eroding moral standards that impact people's lives. It's difficult to watch the decay and not feel sick.

But then we ask ourselves other questions: How would Jesus respond to such things? How would he have responded to Briana? How did he respond to women like her in the first century? This is important, because Jesus is our model. He is completely holy and righteous (1 John 2:1), without sin, the exact likeness of God the Father (Col. 1:15–20). He is not soft on sin, but died so that his children might be free of its penalty (Rom. 5:21). His response will be instructive, healthy, wise, and pure. His response, whatever it is, will help us wage war with sexual temptation in our own lives and in our ministries as we attempt to work together as siblings.

Have you ever noticed that Jesus kept running into bad women—women with infamous reputations and questionable sexual histories? Did they seek him or did he look for them? How did he treat them? And what can we learn from him?

The Soiled Samaritan (John 4:1–26)

Sandra came for pastoral counseling because her relationship with her mother had dogged her for years and she was desperate to be free of her mother's negative influence. She described their relationship as the reverse of most mothers and daughters. Normally the mother models maturity and nurtures her daughter toward wisdom. Instead, Sandra confided in me that she felt more like the parent, constantly cautioning her mother to stop getting involved with bad men. Her mother did not stay with one man longer than a few years. As a result, Sandra never knew her father, and during her formative years, men popped in and out of her life like nut grass. After four messy divorces, her mother determined it would be simpler just to move in—and the latest escapade brought Sandra to my office.

Wild women like Sandra's mother arouse pity and disgust. They are the brunt of off-color jokes. They act like immature adolescents. Unfortunately, they sow more than oats. They leave behind land-mined families. Most of us are sickened by their delinquent behavior. I admit I felt that way as I listened to Sandra.

Perhaps Jesus' disciples thought similarly of the woman at the well in John 4. Preachers tell her story often but seldom do they paint her as a bad girl. They usually talk about Jesus as Living Water. Sometimes they use the passage to illustrate the way Jesus values women, or the sin of racial prejudice, or methods of evangelism. But in all these sermons we have never heard anyone paint this woman as easy, fast, wild, promiscuous, licentious, or oversexed. How would you describe a woman today who has been married five times and is, at this moment, living with someone who is not her husband?

> The woman said to him, "Sir, give me this water so that I won't get thirsty and have to keep coming here to draw water."
> He told her, "Go, call your husband and come back."
> "I have no husband," she replied.
> Jesus said to her, "You are right when you say you have no husband. The fact is, you have had five husbands, and the man you now have is not your husband. What you have just said is quite true." (John 4:15–18)

What is her story? Wouldn't you love to know? What happened to those five men she married? Was she presently living with another woman's husband? Were these forced marriages or was she simply an immoral, loose woman? We don't know. But in a strict Eastern culture, we know this woman was the brunt of town gossip and an outcast of proper society.

Was Jesus' encounter with this woman an accident? We know from the text that it was not. He came looking for her. John writes, "Now he had to go through Samaria" (4:4). Their meeting was carefully orchestrated by a sovereign God.

Jesus, having sent his disciples into town, sits alone at the well, and up saunters a wicked woman. She came to the well in the heat of the day when most women had already drawn water, probably so she would not run into any of them. But Jesus is there and something amazing happens! He is a Jewish man and he asks her to give him a drink—he asks to drink from the same cup as the village bad girl!

Could she have wondered if he was hitting on her? If so, not for long. Jesus does not treat her like a loose woman. He does not proposition her or take advantage of her vulnerability. Jesus experienced temptations like all men do (Heb. 4:15), but he does not see this woman as a potential lover. He sees her as a sister.

He confronts her shame but then gives her a theology lesson. He speaks to her as one capable of learning deep truths and one who is worthy to worship Almighty God. There is nothing sensual in his response to her, and she senses something she has not felt for years—a man's respect and brotherly love. This wholesome, tender sibling kindness changes her forever. Jesus would not play sex games. He could always be trusted to do what was in a woman's best interest.

What happens next is even more astonishing! She runs back to the village and tells everyone about her conversation—and they run out to see Jesus. Verse 39 is surprising: "Many of the Samaritans from that town believed in him because of the woman's testimony." In Eastern cultures women's words were worthless. Women could not be witnesses in a trial.[1] Even chaste women were not considered smart enough or ethical enough to be trustworthy.

What happened that these people listened to her words and believed her? We don't know. Did she say or do something to change people's opinion of her? Did she confess her sins with such power that the people believed they were witnessing a transformed life? Did she move out of her lover's house and vow a new lifestyle? Again, we don't know. But something changed her from the inside out, and it began with the power of a brother's love.

A Sister—Shamed and Stoned, or Sanitized and Safe? (John 8:2–11)

The account of Jesus and the woman caught in adultery is well known, but let's look at it through the eyes of sibling love.[2]

At dawn he appeared again in the temple courts, where all the people gathered around him, and he sat down to teach them. The teachers of the law and the Pharisees brought

in a woman caught in adultery. They made her stand before the group and said to Jesus, "Teacher, this woman was
caught in the act of adultery. In the Law Moses commanded
us to stone such women. Now what do you say?" They were
using this question as a trap, in order to have a basis for ac-
cusing him.

But Jesus bent down and started to write on the ground
with his finger. When they kept on questioning him, he
straightened up and said to them, "If any one of you is without sin, let him be the first to throw a stone at her." Again he
stooped down and wrote on the ground.

At this, those who heard began to go away one at a time,
the older ones first, until only Jesus was left, with the woman
still standing there. Jesus straightened up and asked her,
"Woman, where are they? Has no one condemned you?"

"No one, sir," she said.

"Then neither do I condemn you," Jesus declared. "Go
now and leave your life of sin." (John 8:2–11)

Notice that John makes a point of telling us about Jesus' physical
posture—lots of stooping and standing. Why, one might ask. First
we find that the Jewish leaders drag a woman into the temple courts
in front of Jesus where a large crowd gathers. We observe that she
has been caught in the very act, an act in which one is usually naked.
Did they give her time to get dressed? We doubt it. Was part of the
humiliation to drag her into public exposed? If so, we may have an
explanation for all this stooping and standing, and some insight into
the mysterious question: Why did Jesus write on the ground?

John points out that they made her stand before the group. This
is another indication that she might have been naked. If she were
unclothed, she probably would have wanted to crouch down to cover
herself as much as possible. Making her *stand*—well, you get the
picture!

Imagine the gawking crowd! There she is standing naked while
the Jewish leaders spout the Mosaic Law to Jesus. Actually the lead-

ers misrepresented Leviticus 20:10 and Deuteronomy 22:22–24, which state that in the case of adultery *both* the man and the woman must be put to death, but her accusers conveniently neglected to bring him along. They ask Jesus what to do with her, hoping to trap him. If he condemns her, he will lose favor with the people. If he does not, he will be disagreeing with Moses.

Jesus did not respond to their question verbally but instead bent down on the ground and wrote something in the dust with his finger. For centuries, Bible scholars have been trying to guess what he was doing down there. Actually it's impossible to know for sure—but what if Jesus' intent was not about what he was writing? What if he was focusing the crowd's eyes on his hand and off her body? What if you were standing naked? Would you appreciate a refocusing off your genitals? We know we would. This could be the action of a big brother attempting to alleviate his sister's embarrassment, a unique way of covering her up.

After writing in the dust, Jesus stood up to face his adversaries: "If any one of you is without sin, let him be the first to throw a stone at her." Then he stooped down again and moved his finger in the dust . . . eyes focused there one more time, instead of on his sister. The crowd walks away one by one, beginning with her accusers. Finally, when only the two of them are left, he is still stooped, looking down, and she alone is standing in the temple court. Now he stands up and this time he turns to her, and (most likely, in keeping with his character) looks straight into her dazed eyes. *Where are they? Has no one condemned you? Then neither do I, but go and leave this life behind. It only leads to humiliation and pain. Free yourself and live worthy of who you are, my sister.* He alone was without sin, so he alone could forgive her and release her to a new life of hope and purity.[3]

Sometimes erroneously identified as Mary Magdalene, this woman—whoever she was—represents promiscuous women throughout the ages.[4] We don't know her specific circumstances. We don't know if she was looking for love in all the wrong places or if somehow she was coerced. Women without male advocates were often forced into prostitution to live. Others were "bad girls." We do know that misuse and distortion of God's beautiful gift of sexuality has been a source of sin and pain for men and women since the fall.

But Jesus refused to take advantage of her sin or misfortune, whichever it was. He did not mock her, laugh at her, or make jokes about her. Instead, he modeled a brother's love. He set an example of integrity for all of us to follow. He could have seen her as a seductive woman, but he chose to see her first as a person who needed God. He had her best interest at heart. He chose to see her through the eyes of a protective big brother. Neither did he make light of her sin. He instructed her to leave her promiscuous lifestyle and pursue purity and wholeness, commensurate with her identity as a child of the Father.

Did she become his disciple? Odds are she did. Who can resist such love? The gospel attracted women in the early church days. Women flock to Jesus today because of this love, and women will flock to ministries led by men and women who treat one another with this kind of unconditional love and bold instruction. What a beautiful picture of sibling love!

A Foot Massage at Dinner (Luke 7:36–50)

Imagine dinner on the veranda at the home of a wealthy and prominent community leader. Passersby drink in delicious smells of gourmet cuisine and wish for an invitation. Selected guests arrive and are greeted with courtesies appropriate for their station in life, a kiss on the cheek, a bit of oil on the head, some water to wash away the dust from the street. All are honored with these Eastern tokens of respect—except one. One of the invited guests is snubbed, not privileged to the finery afforded the others. But he does not make a scene. He is Jesus, and Jesus is a gentleman.

Why has he been invited? Only Simon the Pharisee could tell us. Perhaps it was to set him up with a trick question or two, hoping to stump and embarrass him. He is, after all, the topic of gossip in these circles. Why not invite him and see what happens? But the unexpected happens.

When a woman who had lived a sinful life in that town learned that Jesus was eating at the Pharisee's house, she brought an alabaster jar of perfume, and as she stood behind him at his feet weeping, she began to wet his feet with her tears. Then she wiped them with her hair, kissed them and poured perfume on them.

When the Pharisee who had invited him saw this, he said to himself, "If this man were a prophet, he would know who is touching him and what kind of woman she is—that she is a sinner." (Luke 7:37–39)

An uninvited guest shows up. It's the town prostitute, and, of course, they don't give her a place at the table. She's not interested in joining the celebration anyway. She has come looking for Jesus. And she sees him among the guests.

Why has she come looking for Jesus? We can speculate that she was in the crowd earlier and something about him prompted her to leave her nightly work, buy perfume she could not afford, and find him. What did she plan to do with her gift? Pouring scented oil on another was a sign of utmost respect, submission, and affection. What had Jesus said or done to bring about such extravagance? Onlookers might assume she was enamored with him, seeking a client. But the opposite was true. Here was a man who did not see her as a harlot. Here was a man who saw her as a sister. She sensed he cared for her as a person in the *imago dei* (image of God), and her response was intense, almost reckless. In him, she saw hope for new life—a different kind of life. So she set out to find him.

It's a warm night and they are reclining on sofas, sprawled out on their sides, sharing delicacies from a central table. Jesus' feet just happen to be within her reach. So when she found him, she simply stood at his feet unable to stop crying. There are no words recorded— just tears and physical expressions. Were they tears of sadness over the way she was living? Were they tears of joy mixed with hope of change? Maybe both? The Bible doesn't say. First, she stands, then kneels to kiss and massage his feet, wet with her tears. Finally she breaks the vase and pours the aromatic oil all over his feet, rubbing in the oil with her hands and hair.

Let me (Sue) break in with a little commentary on foot massages. I am sixty, and my kids have been after me for years to get a massage—and I resisted until a few months ago. For some reason, maybe as a treat or to relieve stress, I decided to try a professional massage. Wow! I signed up for a year. While a massage is relaxing, it is also sensual enough to make me feel it's more appropriate from someone of my own gender. Even a foot massage could break down one's resistance to greater physical contact if one were not careful. Simon the Pharisee probably thought along the same lines as he saw this woman massaging Jesus' feet. *She's touching him. If he were a godly man, he would not let her.*

Jesus is not turned on by this woman's intimate gestures. Again, he sees her heart and treats her as a sister. He rebukes Simon for his rude behavior and arrogant attitude toward his own sin. And he affirms this woman's actions as an honorable gift of sibling love.

> "Do you see this woman? I came into your house. You did not give me any water for my feet, but she wet my feet with her tears and wiped them with her hair. You did not give me a kiss, but this woman, from the time I entered, has not stopped kissing my feet. You did not put oil on my head, but she has poured perfume on my feet. Therefore, I tell you, her many sins have been forgiven—for she loved much. . . ."
>
> Jesus said to the woman, "Your faith has saved you; go in peace." (Luke 7:44–47, 50)

He sent her on her way with the gift of a new life, a life full of peace, joy, and purity—for there is no inner peace without purity. Her life was changed forever because Jesus saw who she could be and acted like a brother.

I've not lived cautiously. I have friendships with women. I touch them. I've been more careful in school than I was in the parish, where everyone knows me. It's different now because someone can come to my office and we can have a deep talk and the next day I won't know his or her name. That didn't happen in a church setting. So I'm more careful now. But I'm not obsessive. These are my friends. Touch is a human thing, not just a sexual thing. It is dehumanizing to deny touch. Is sex a contagious disease? Sex is a danger, but money is a danger too. Do you refuse to take a salary because money is a danger?

I am convinced that the so-called failures in ministry are not motivated sexually. For both men and women, they are motivated by arrogance, pride, power, and a hunger for intimacy. It doesn't happen overnight. They have long histories before them. The failures don't happen because you touch somebody. They have to do with character development—part of learning to be a man or a woman. It's part of spiritual maturity and spiritual formation.

—Dr. Eugene Peterson[5]

Wild Women, Come to Church?

Eating breakfast with Briana and thinking about Jesus' interaction with these three wild women reminded me of the opening story in Philip Yancey's book *What's So Amazing About Grace?* He heard it from a friend who worked with addicts and street women in Chicago.

A prostitute came to me in wretched straits, homeless, sick, unable to buy food for her two-year-old daughter. Through sobs and tears, she told me she had been renting out her daughter—two years old!—to men interested in kinky sex. She made more renting out her daughter for an hour than she could earn on her own in a night. She had to do it, she said, to support her own drug habit. I could hardly bear hearing her sordid story. For one thing, it made me legally liable—I'm required to report cases of child abuse. I had no idea what to say to this woman.

At last I asked if she had ever thought of going to a church for help. I will never forget the look of pure, naïve shock that crossed her face. "Church!" she cried. "Why would I ever go there? I was already feeling terrible about myself. They'd just make me feel worse."[6]

Yancey writes, "What struck me about my friend's story is that women much like this prostitute fled toward Jesus, not away from him. The worse a person felt about herself, the more likely she saw Jesus as a refuge. Has the church lost that gift? Evidently the down and out, who flocked to Jesus when he lived on earth, no longer feel welcome among his followers. What has happened?"[7]

Yancey's question indicts the church today. I (Henry) have seen Yancey's story in my own life. Seven years ago I helped a former stripper named Amy. After years of working in the porn industry, she had finally found the courage to walk into a church to find help. Way out of her comfort zone at the time, Amy confided, "I felt like the walls were about to cave in on me." Thankfully, Amy was received by the church with open arms and was cared for as she began her season of healing.

A few years after I met Amy, I came in contact with a woman named Maya who also had worked in sexually oriented businesses. After discussions with my assistant, Landra, I hired Maya to work with us in the chaplain's department doing clerical work. Under Landra's supervision, Maya worked with us for several months as she got back on her feet. When Maya worked for me, I didn't see a woman who had made her living using her body. I saw a woman created in the image of God who had lost her way. She was the prize who needed the Savior.

When Jesus interacted with bad girls in the Bible, he changed their lives. God has called the church to do the same thing today.

And if we can be used by God to reach women like Amy and Maya, shouldn't we be able to work with each other without our sexuality getting in the way? If men and women cannot work together in ministry, how are we ever going to be able to help women like Amy and Maya? The good news is that we can certainly work together and God can use us to reach the wild men and women of our day!

As we work together, we need wisdom and discernment. In the next chapter we will explore a strategy that will help brothers and sisters effectively manage sibling relationships.

DISCUSSION QUESTIONS

1. Have you ever known anyone who lived a promiscuous lifestyle or worked in the sex industry? (No names, please!) If so, describe them to the group. How did you feel toward this person?
2. How do you feel about pornographers and pimps? What is your gut response if you see them on television or in a film?
3. Describe your reaction to suggestive magazines that greet you in the grocery checkout line.
4. Why do you think Jesus kept running into "bad" women?
5. Respond to the three accounts of Jesus with "wild women." Were any of the accounts particularly meaningful to you? If so, why?
6. What was Jesus' response to "wild women"? What is yours? What can we learn from Jesus? What tensions come to mind?

Chapter 12

Color-Coded Attractions

Help your brother's boat across, and your own will reach the shore.
—HINDU PROVERB

IN AN AGE OF TERRORISM, THE U.S. government installed a color-coded alarm system to alert us to the threat of enemy attack—from red for severe risk, down to green for low. They know that there are seasons when we need to be particularly diligent related to our security, but our responses should be based on solid evidence. It is foolish and wasteful to be on red alert all the time.

Sexual attractions can also be color-coded. Fortunately, none of us is attracted to everyone. Some have assumed that everyone is severe risk, and as a result, like the Pharisees or the Taliban, have outlawed working with the opposite sex altogether. They are on red alert all the time. Of course those with special addictions should adopt a "constant red alert" strategy—but that's not everyone. We established that Jesus and Paul worked alongside women in the first century. Banning women from ministry because of sexual temptation is not God's way, and it eliminates over half the workforce. But we need a battle plan—in fact we need several.

Color-Coded Battle Plans

Some mixed-gender relationships signal green alert, low risk. Your friend's ninety-year-old grandmother probably won't be a danger for most men under eighty. If a woman works with a man she finds unappealing, he is not likely to show up in her dreams. There are green alert people who drift in and out of our lives and they don't pose much danger. Our goal as brothers and sisters is to see everyone as green.

However, attractions are tricky. We don't wake up in the morning and say, "I think I'll have an affair today." It happens over time and with people that surprise us. So the code blue alert, "guarded," is a wise plan of action with most people we work with. Guarded doesn't mean we act silly, building fences that squelch a healthy sibling friendship. (We will discuss appropriate fences in the next chapter.) Guarded means we use sound judgment as we interact.

The other colors, yellow, orange, and red alerts, differ for men and women and for individuals within the same gender, but all require serious attention. Various factors come into play—emotional and spiritual health, maturity, previous struggles, temperament, vulnerability to the visual, and so on.

For example, individuals within each gender respond differently to people who *really* look good to them—known as "eye candy." Remember some of us love Reese's Peanut Butter Cups and others relish Snickers, but we all know that seemingly irresistible feeling that we can't stop looking. A brother describes how he feels around "eye candy."

> To be very honest, really attractive women make me uncomfortable. Not because they intimidate me, but because (a) I worry about staring at them and (b) I worry about what others might think. Now let me clarify . . . I am not stupid, so I am not worried about giving attractive women these sleazy, lustful looks. I am not going to do that. What I am worried about is just the simple, observational looks of, "Wow, she is really pretty" that you can't stop doing and

having this person notice those looks and feel uncomfortable. I think if you ask most guys they would recognize the
difference between a lustful stare and this other look I am
trying to describe, and they would hopefully agree that they
are also uncomfortable around really attractive women. If
not, I'm going to feel like a dork. Also I worry about other
people thinking that something more than work is going on
or my wife worrying about something.[1]

Reading this brother's honest confession should help sisters carefully consider how they present themselves in public, another topic
we will tackle later in depth. In addition, think about the advantage
for the majority of us who are not "eye candy." I (Sue), as a seminary professor, teach and work with men constantly, and, upon hearing my brother's words, realized that being exceptionally attractive
would be a detriment in my work. I want my students to be thinking
about the topic I'm teaching, and not looking at me.

Sisters, consider that exceptional beauty has a downside. If you
envy beautiful women or spend too much time trying to be like them,
remember God can use your appearance in whatever he calls you
to do (see Ps. 139:13–16). Take care of yourself, look pleasing—but
abandon the typical, absurd American obsession with appearance.

For some men, and even a few women, intense physical attractions are a constant battle, requiring automatic and constant red
alert in all mixed-gender settings. If you fall under this category,
find someone trustworthy in whom you can confide, and consider
accepting the help of professionals.[2] You should work hard for emotional health before assuming influential ministry positions where
you could use your power to take advantage of others or defame the
Lord. Self-control is mandatory for ministry leaders.

Since an overseer is entrusted with God's work, he must be
blameless—not overbearing, not quick-tempered, not given
to drunkenness, not violent, not pursuing dishonest gain.
Rather he must be hospitable, *one who loves what is good*, who

is *self-controlled, upright, holy and disciplined.* (Titus 1:7–8, italics added)

For others "eye candy" calls for an SOS prayer and a concerted effort at self-talk, remembering that even this attractive man or woman is a person first, a creature Jesus loves dearly, and someone deserving respect and kindness. A mature brother has his sister's best interest at heart, even if she looks good, and will submit his fleshly desires to Jesus, asking for the fruit of the Spirit to be evident in his life. And for many women, the old adage "beauty is only skin deep" applies to the men they see. To take her to the next alert level, it would require more than eye appeal—it demands a relational element.

Because of the complexity of the issue and individuals, God does not give us a formula or rule book, although many try to implement one, hoping for a guarantee. He asks us to develop a heart like his. Following a formula is the Pharisee way—not the Jesus way. Our task is more complicated. Know yourself and what moves you up the alert ladder. Just as Homeland Security takes precautionary steps to deal with a raised alert, we must be alert and wise—especially as we work in mixed-gender teams—but not at the expense of community.

Although there is no rule book, there are principles and guidelines. This is not a book about sex. There are excellent books already written on that topic, but sexual temptation affects our topic—relationships between sisters and brothers in ministry—so we need to think about it in that context. What do brothers and sisters need to consider as they work together?

Sexual Attractions Are Normal

An old hermit and his son lived far back in the mountains, away from any other human beings. The boy had never seen another person besides his father. Finally, the old hermit decided to take the boy into town on his birthday to give him his first taste of civilization. Walking down the street, they passed a couple of pretty girls and the boy said, "What in the world are those?"

The old hermit was caught off guard. "Er, uh, that's nothing, son,"

he said. "Just a couple of geese." The boy seemed to accept the explanation, so they went on. The pair spent a full day browsing around
town, visiting different shops. . . the livery stables, the sawmill, the
blacksmith shop. At last they decided to head home. But before they
left, the old hermit asked, "Son, I'd like to get you a birthday present. Did you see anything here that you'd like to have?"

"Sure!" the boy said, "I want a couple of geese!"[3]

God created sex and the human sex drive. Both are good. He designed us male and female, intending that we would be attracted
to each other. It's time to stop hiding that reality and talk about
attractions honestly. We are all drawn—the question is what do we
do with that magnetism? We are drawn to many things—food, adventure, pleasure, stuff—but maturity is learning to control these
desires. The same goes for sexual temptation. Some Christians believe the sex drive is evil and try to repress or ignore it. That is why
sex is the taboo subject in so many churches—and it has been for
centuries. Where did this idea come from?

Blame theologians like Augustine and Luther. We laud their
many fine contributions to theology but lament their views on sexuality. Augustine believed that sex apart from sinful lust was impossible, and that one must avoid sex altogether to escape from such
sin.[4] The practice of celibacy for church leaders grew out of this idea,
and the practice is still a source of dissension and disagreement in
Catholicism today.[5]

Sexual prohibition was one of the first doctrines that Martin
Luther and the other Reformers left behind in protest.[6] But even
Martin Luther had his hang-ups: "Intercourse is never without sin;
but God excuses it by his grace because the estate of marriage is his
work."[7] Augustinian thinking still influences the church today, thus
our taboo topic leaves many Christians in denial or mum when they
struggle with sexual attractions.

Linda Dillow and Lorraine Pintus have helped thousands of
women overcome sexual inhibitions and distorted thinking. Sisters,
if you need frank balanced advice and instruction on healthy sexuality, read *Intimate Issues* or attend one of their conferences.[8] At a retreat

they asked seventeen women in church leadership and two hundred fifty women attendees, "Have you ever found yourself attracted to another man?" The results were surprising.

> What percent of these godly women do you think said yes? Fifty percent? Seventy percent? No. Ninety percent admitted to feeling attracted to another man. (For all we know, the other ten percent are either fibbing or newly married!) These statistics shocked Shelly [a woman we were counseling] when we shared them with her. "If this is such a common problem, why isn't anyone talking about it?" People do talk about it—after the fact. We talk about the prominent pastors, evangelists, and singers who have fallen into sexual sin. We talk about the couple across the street who is getting a divorce because one partner had an affair. We talk about how tragic it is for the children and the faithful spouse. We discuss the impact of infidelity: the house for sale, the ministry in ruins, the church with empty seats.[9]

Yes, we talk, but too late. Let's admit that sexual attractions are normal, for both men and women.

Proverbial Wisdom

Agur, the author of Proverbs 30, described sexual tension in colorful pictures.

> There are three things that are too amazing for me,
> four I do not understand:
> the way of an eagle in the sky,
> the way of a snake on a rock,
> the way of a ship on the high seas,
> and the way of a man with a maiden.
> (Prov. 30:18–19)

What do these four things have in common? They are all mysterious and fascinating to watch. They all involve movement. The emphasis is on the last example—the way of a man with a maiden. Romantic themed films and books continue to top best-seller lists and make money. A chemistry bubbles up and charms us. Sparks fly, shackling our common sense. Teenagers are mostly in love with love—silly and giddy. This attraction is powerful—God designed it that way—but, like uncontained fire, it can also be dangerous.

The proverb that follows verses 18 and 19 paints a stark contrast, showing us what happens when the enemy has the opportunity to distort God's gift of healthy sexuality. Instead of the way of a man with a maid, it is the way of an immoral woman with an immoral man.

> This is the way of the adulteress:
> She eats and wipes her mouth
> and says, "I've done nothing wrong."
> (Prov. 30:20)

No mystery. The picture is not winsome or beautiful. The adulteress partakes of pleasure and then wipes her mouth. The feel is coarse, crass, vulgar, and unrefined. And she's defensive: "I've done nothing wrong. Don't bother me, you prude!"

Through imagery and contrast, Solomon captures the tension we live in every day. Something compels us as we observe the way of a man with a maid. It's warm, fun, beautiful, and affirming. It feels right. Getting married or growing older doesn't change our DNA. Although we should become more seasoned and wise in our responses over time, attractions never completely go away.

Sue's Story

When I (Sue) was in the third grade, I was attracted to Richard Gilreath. I don't remember much about him, except that he had wavy blond hair and I thought he was divine. Through the years, I was drawn to different boys, and later men—and they did not have much in common. I cannot give you any rational reason why them and not others. I simply saw them and suddenly I felt a romantic yearning. I began to think about them differently from other people. I hoped to see them again. I hoped they might show a personal interest in me. Sometimes that thing called "chemistry" overrode good sense. Fortunately, I was not drawn to bad men, as some women are, and through God's protection and grace, I married a fine godly man, chemistry intact.

After we married, I never expected to feel any physical attraction for anyone besides my husband. But I was wrong. And my background made me a prime candidate for problems. In my home, sex was *the* taboo subject. I learned about it from misinformed playground friends and I carried some absurd notions about sex for years.

When I joined God's family in my mid-twenties, I learned to fear sexual temptation as the thing that could ruin our marriage and destroy our lives. Every week I studied the Bible with women, discussing all kinds of personal topics—even sex in marriage—but never sexual temptation outside of marriage. It was assumed that "good" Christian women did not struggle with attractions.

Even though my husband and I have a good marriage, with normal ups and downs, several times during our marriage I felt romantic feelings toward other men—a neighbor, a man in our home group. I was able to "manage" these attractions by myself—but I never dared tell anyone. I was too ashamed. I simply wrestled with my thoughts and they subsided—until my daughter's senior year in high school.

I was president of the PTA and I found myself strangely attracted to the principal, a good Christian man. I couldn't believe it! The first week of school, I moved up the alert ladder into the red zone—danger sounded and red lights flashed. I knew I would be forced to work with this man all year to carry out my duties—and I could see the headlines: "PTA President and Principal Caught in Torrid Affair."

I knew myself well enough to identify what was happening, and, praise God, I was emotionally healthy enough to have a red-alert battle plan ready. It's critical to know what to do when we find ourselves attracted to a brother or sister in ministry. I did not need my red-alert plan every day around my brothers—just this brother.

What did I do? I did not want to embarrass my children by re-
signing before I even began to fulfill my commitment. What was my
battle plan for the principal—my red-alert plan? Before I tell you,
let's examine the process that can take any of us up the alert ladder
and down the spiral described in the Bible.

The Downward Spiral

James, the half brother of Jesus and leader of the Jerusalem
church, helps us understand, battle, and conquer sexual sin—all required if we are to work together as siblings.

> Let no one say when he is tempted, "I am tempted by God,"
> for God cannot be tempted by evil, and he himself tempts
> no one. But each one is tempted when he is lured and en-
> ticed by his own desires. Then when desire conceives, it
> gives birth to sin, and when sin is full grown, it gives birth
> to death. Do not be led astray, my dear brothers and sisters.
> All generous giving and every perfect gift is from above,
> coming down from the Father of lights, with whom there is
> no variation or the slightest hint of change. By his sovereign
> plan he gave us birth through the message of truth, that
> we would be a kind of firstfruits of all he created. (James
> 1:13–18 NET)

James's downward spiral contains identifiable stages that can save
us from the plunge: first attraction, then deliberation, and finally
consummation.

Step 1: Attraction

It begins with that initial attraction that we talked about. It happens to everyone. Sometimes it ambushes us out of nowhere. And it
is not sin. It is part of being human—the way God designed each of
us. Male or female, married or single, young or old—we all experience attractions.

Maybe your wife struggles with her weight and your ministry

partner, Mary, works out every day, taking great pride in her fitness. And you catch yourself thinking, "Wow—I love the way Mary takes care of herself." You admire Mary and you wonder what it would be like to be more intimate with her. Stop—you are moving up the alert ladder. Go no further—don't cross that line!

> For though we live as human beings, we do not wage war according to human standards, for the weapons of our warfare are not human weapons, but are made powerful by God for tearing down strongholds. We tear down arguments and every arrogant obstacle that is raised up against the knowledge of God, and we take every thought captive to make it obey Christ. (2 Cor. 10:3–5 NET)

That thought comparing your wife to your coworker, that's the thought you can—and must—take captive. Make it obey Christ. What would Christ have you do with it? How can you honor him with your eyes and mind? Jesus says, "my son, see Mary as your sister. She is off-limits. You don't lust after your sister in the faith family! It's unthinkable. You have Mary's best interest at heart. You are her brother and, as her brother, you don't want Mary entangled with a married man."

Then replace those earlier thoughts about Mary with good thoughts about your wife—the woman you promised in a solemn covenant to honor and love above all others. You think about your children, and your love for your Lord—and how all those things have eternal value. Compare that to a few pounds of flesh and regain your perspective.

> I have a daughter who is quite attractive, but I have to wash that through, "She's my daughter." When working with women, the same principle applies—"Wait a minute, she's my sister." The metaphor helps a lot.
>
> —Steve Roese

In our experience, each time you take that thought captive before it takes hold of you, it will be easier next time. Ultimately you will find that you struggle less and less. You may be able to work with Mary, although you will always have to be more careful with her than with other women. Mary should not be penalized because of your attraction. She should not even know. Of course, we are assuming that Mary is acting like a sister. What if she acts inappropriately? Brothers, you are still not off the hook. We will address Mary's responsibilities in the modesty chapter. But even if she is not acting like a sister, you are called to love her like one. Jesus modeled sibling love for all women—even the promiscuous ones. Jesus asks you to love her like a sister, with a brother's protective care.

Our desire, as brothers and sisters in Christ, is to stop the spiral in this stage—and we can. But, let's say that, for some reason, we don't. Then we continue deeper and deeper down the spiral of tempta tion—or higher and higher up the ladder of alert levels, whichever metaphor you prefer. Attraction and temptation are not sin, but the next step is.

Step 2: Deliberation

Sharon and Manuel looked forward to Sundays when they helped out in the Hispanic inner-city church, sponsored by their suburban congregation. They loved young people, the opportunity to prac tice their Spanish, and the ministry team's camaraderie. Sharon's husband, Philip, preferred to attend the early service at the mother church, allowing him to get home in time to catch golf on TV. Sha ron found herself admiring Manuel and wishing Philip were more like him. "He's sold out to Jesus, I can really talk to him, and he is such a good listener. I wish Philip . . ." And she began to entertain thoughts of a more intimate nature. Red alert! Red lights flashing. She ignored them.

> We give some practical advice that is not legalistic but
> still effective. First of all, understand the power of human
> sexuality. Probably 80 percent of our discipline cases
> have some component of sexual error in it, so we have
> a healthy regard and respect for it. We don't say, "Let's
> pretend it's not there." The second thing is that we realize
> in many ways that the bedroom is the end game. If you
> are having conversations with someone other than your
> spouse at an intimacy level that is deeper than what you
> have with your spouse—that's where you are crossing a
> line. So we tell people that conversation matters, and en-
> courage them to keep it on a level less intimate than you
> would with your spouse. If you find yourself falling into that
> direction with someone because the ministry relationship
> is close, you have to pull back.
>
> —Elizabeth Maring[10]

Each Sunday she looked forward to seeing Manuel. The Sundays
he had to work, she came home in a bad mood. She stood a little
closer to him than the other workers. She sat next to him in the
debriefing. This is what James calls being "lured and enticed by
[our] own desires" (James 1:14 NET). He calls this process "desire
conceiving." What is being conceived? Something very dangerous.
She is giving herself permission to dwell on wrong thoughts and
rationalize wrong choices. She may not be sleeping with Manuel,
but she is already in the initial stages of an emotional affair. The red
lights are flashing but she is ignoring them. This is sin.

Step 3: Consummation

"It seems silly to waste gas. Why don't we carpool?" suggests Sharon. If Manuel chooses not to act like a brother, he will agree and
the spiral will suck them both down. They are setting themselves
up for easy sin, and in time, they will probably act on what they are
feeling.

James says this sister and brother are giving "birth to sin, and when [that] sin is full grown, it gives birth to death" (James 1:15 NET). If we toy with temptation, we find that, with lightning speed, and sometimes almost out of nowhere, we have crossed the line and are engaging in sexual sin. We go under. And James says we will suffocate on the consequences. What dies? Many things—marriages, ministries, integrity, and our spiritual lives, because we cannot knowingly sin and remain close to Jesus. We step away in shame. This spiral sucks us down because we did not have a red alert plan and act on it!

Solutions

In our nation, emotional and physical affairs are played out countless times every day. For Christians, sexual sin is especially inappropriate because God calls us to see and treat one another as siblings in God's family. Did I (Sue) commit adultery with the principal I told you about earlier? No, by God's grace, I was able to stop the spiral when the red lights began to flash. But because I was in the midst of a real battle, I took some drastic steps to protect myself. I was willing to step down from my responsibilities as PTA president, but I hoped to find a creative alternative.

I did. I became a world-class delegator. I found other moms to take over the majority of projects where he was directly involved. When I interacted with him, I kept it professional and focused on the task at hand. I did not attend the state PTA conference because it required that I travel with him, and I knew that would be foolish. I found ways to do my job with very little contact, and it was a great year for the PTA. I found that as the year progressed, the attraction waned, but if my plan had not worked, I was prepared to resign.

Should you continue to work with a brother or sister to whom you are attracted? Each situation is different. If you find yourself moving into the red zone, short on self-control, be prepared to take drastic action. If it means quitting the ministry, do it. If it means changing ministry partners, try that. But remember God is able to keep your foot from stumbling. Of course, you have to do your part. Fight first, fight hard—but if you are slipping, flee.

I (Sue) have found that, as I have grown closer to the Lord, these attractions have lost their power. This does not mean that I am invincible. I must stay on guard just like everyone else. But it does mean that Jesus is able, as we entrust ourselves to him, to help us love our siblings, like he did—with a holy love.

We have looked at the way Jesus loved everyone—even promiscuous people. We have examined the graded alert system to help us manage attractions. And we have observed James's downward spiral to protect us from sexual sin with siblings. But what are the everyday fences we need to build to provide a loving, yet safe, environment to work with our brothers and sisters? That is the subject of the next chapter.

DISCUSSION QUESTIONS

1. Respond to the idea of color-coded attractions presented in the chapter. How can we be wise in our relationships while creating healthy mixed-gender community?

2. (For men only!) Reread the quote from Scott on pages 175–76. Can you relate to this brother's words? How do you deal with similar incidents?

3. What have you done to protect yourself when you were strangely attracted to someone?

4. What coaching would you give someone who came to you for counseling about their battle with sexual attractions?

5. Do you agree that only emotionally healthy men and women should pursue influential ministry positions? Discuss.

6. How does James's advice about sin in 1:13–18 relate to sexual temptation?

7. What advice would you offer anyone who has moved past attraction and into deliberation or consummation?

Chapter 13

Wise Boundaries and Fences

It's me, it's me, it's me, O Lawd,
Standin' in de need o' prayer.
T'aint my brother, t'aint my sister,
But it's me, O Lawd,
Standin' in de need o' prayer.
—WILLIAM REDDICK

ONE STORMY DALLAS EVENING, I (Henry) waited for my two guests to arrive at my office. I had been invited to appear on a local television show to discuss my book *The Silent War*, which deals with the pornography plague that is a huge problem for many guys today.[1] My two guests would appear on the show with me. One of my guests was a guy who had struggled with porn, and he would share his story on the show. My other guest was a former topless dancer who had recently left the porn industry. Our plan was to meet at my office and drive to the studio together with dinner on the way. It sounded like a good plan to me until the phone rang . . .

When I answered the phone, I heard the frantic voice of the guy who was to appear with me. It seems that rainwater had flooded his house and he would not be able to make it. When I hung up the phone, it rang again. The former stripper was in the lobby. As I went to meet her, it dawned on me that I would be going out to dinner with a woman who used to take her clothes off for men. If my wife had been there, I doubt she would have waved as we drove off saying, "Have a good time!" I felt like I was in a no-win situation. I decided to go with the plan we had agreed on.

To make matters worse, at dinner she began to tell me that she was having trouble in her marriage. I can't remember what I said, but I do remember wishing that the evening would end quickly.

You would think that I would finally learn my lesson . . . but sometimes I need to learn a lesson more than once to make it stick. Several months later I was invited by Christian recording artist Al Denson to fly on a private plane to Missouri to see the work he was doing in public schools. Three others would be on the flight, and Al asked me to invite my boss. He couldn't make it, so I invited my assistant Jenny, who had worked with me for six years.

We left in the morning and drove out together to the airfield. It was a long day with the plane arriving back in Dallas at almost midnight. After a forty-five-minute drive, we pulled into the parking garage at work as one of the night crew was coming in. As soon as we saw him Jenny and I both said, "uh-oh . . ." Of course we hadn't done anything wrong, but it looked horrible. Here I was driving into the parking garage with my assistant after midnight. I felt like rolling the window down and telling this guy that we had been with a Christian singer all day.

Well, both of those instances made me think about fences as I work and serve with members of the opposite sex. Fences, hedges, boundaries . . . they are all the same thing. I'm talking about defining the relationship.

In the situations above I wasn't worried about making a bad choice, but I hated the way things looked. Can you imagine what would have happened if someone from church or work had walked up to me while I was eating dinner with a former stripper? What would I say? "Oh hi, good to see you! This is my friend Tiffany . . . we're doing a television show tonight on pornography. Oh, Kathy?

Why, yes, she's fine. She's at home with the kids. . . ." Yes, I need fences and so do you.

Building Fences

Once a year I get to see the Dallas Mavericks play. The seats are great and the American Airlines Center is a beautiful place. When I look down on the court, it is easy to see the lines that make a basketball court. The lines are two inches in width and they mark the out-of-bounds, half-court, and three-point line. The lines even form something called "the key." In the National Basketball Association, the regulation court dimension is ninety-four feet long and fifty feet wide. In basketball, the boundaries are very specific and very clear.

Every sport has boundaries of some sort. Tennis, football, soccer, baseball . . . you get the point. So why do they have all the boundaries? Simple . . . it makes the game fun. If you take away the lines, all you have left is chaos. I once saw a news clip of a basketball game where players crossed the boundaries and went into the stands. The game was on the verge of turning into a riot. The sporting event was no longer fun as fans were grabbing children and running for the doors.

As men and women work and serve together, the relationship can be very fruitful. And yes, men and women can be friends, but it is imperative that the relationship is defined. We need to build fences, grow hedges, and set boundaries, because if we don't, we will find chaos at our doorstep.

Some of you reading this may be thinking that I am making a big deal out of nothing. Maybe you don't think you need fences to have a healthy relationship with a member of the opposite sex. Unfortunately, I could spend the rest of this chapter reviewing sad stories from people who felt the same way . . . people who have lost their jobs, left the ministry, and whose marriages ended in divorce.

The apostle Paul clearly warns us in 1 Corinthians 10:12, "Therefore let him who thinks he stands take heed that he does not fall" (NASB). It sounds like Paul wants us to pay attention to situations that could cause our downfall. We would be wise to heed his counsel.

I had a friend in Colorado who graduated from seminary and got a position at the church where he and his wife had been attending. He served on a wonderful staff with several men and one woman. As the months passed, he spent a lot of office time with the woman who was the head of the children's ministry. Office time later turned into late hours. Tragically, neither is now serving in full-time ministry. Both are working to rebuild marriages that were on the brink of destruction.

How could something like this happen? Do you remember the answer to that old question, "How do you eat an elephant?" One bite at a time. I've never had a woman I worked with walk up to me and say, "Hey Henry, I'd like to commit adultery with you." Nope, it's never happened. And it won't happen that way. It will begin with something innocent . . . one bite at a time. That's why I need fences.

In building fences, author John Ortberg uses three tests:

- First, the *Sibling Test*—he asks, "Do I trust this woman as I would my sister?" Ortberg knows that you can't trust every woman. There are some needy, emotionally immature women who need Jesus, and men need to be discerning enough to entrust their care to seasoned female staff members.
- Second, the *Screen Test*—he asks, "Would I be embarrassed if any of our conversations or actions were on a movie screen?"
- Thirdly, the *Secret Test*—"Am I keeping anything secret from my wife?"[2]

Obviously Ortberg writes from a male perspective; however, these tests easily transfer to women as well. Women, ask yourselves, Do I trust this man as I would my brother? Am I keeping any secrets from my husband?

As you work with the opposite sex, how do you fare with the tests? If you are like me, I wish I could say that I always pass each one with flying colors . . . but I don't. Again, I need fences and I know you do too.

Ready to Build?

If you would allow me to coach you a bit, I'd love to share some fences that I have built in my life. They are fences that allow me to have healthy and fruitful relationships with the women I work and serve with. My fences were built and tested over many years . . . and they work. Sisters, although I am sharing from my male perspective, the following principles apply to you, too, so forgive my one-sided terminology and do the mental gymnastics when necessary.

Introduce Your Spouse

When I begin a new working relationship with a woman, I find a way to bring my wife and family into conversations. It's easy to do on Mondays as you recap the weekend around the water cooler.

Unfortunately, I think we send the wrong message when we never mention our spouses in causal conversations . . . whether we mean to or not. We talk about the things that matter to us. Your spouse and family matter, so bring them up on occasion.

Ask your coworkers about their family too. Look for positive things to say about them. Even if you are single, it's very easy to ask about your coworker's family.

It's Time to Hush

It makes good sense to talk about your family with a member of the opposite sex at work, but it makes no sense to discuss problems in your marriage with them. I knew of one man who said a woman at work was helpful to him in trying to understand his wife and their marital problems. He didn't listen when he was told he would be wise to break off the relationship. He is now married to that woman, having left his wife and children.

If you are having trouble in your marriage, find a good friend of the same sex or go to a Christian counselor.

A Picture Is Worth a Thousand Words

Another good idea is keeping a picture of your spouse on your desk. I have two pictures of my wife in my office and it's nice to see her face during the day. I also send a message that I am happily married and my wife matters to me.

> I don't go out to lunch with just one woman. I will go out with a group of people or even multiple women, but not with one woman. I want to avoid the look of impropriety, I want to avoid any potential opportunities, and I don't want to give my wife anything to ever even worry about.
>
> I try not to get into deep emotional conversations with ladies when I am alone with them. These situations have arisen in the past, and, wanting to be compassionate, I will talk to them for a while to show that I care about their problems. But eventually I always suggest they talk to my wife because she is much more compassionate than I am. This is a genuine suggestion, but it is also a convenient excuse to cut our conversation off.
>
> Finally, these things aren't just to protect my wife, they are to protect me from me. I don't think anyone ever wakes up and decides, "I think I am going to have an affair today." It is something that happens gradually. Well, as much as I love my wife and want to be a holy and righteous man, I would be a fool to think that I am immune to these same temptations. Therefore, I just want to avoid giving myself the opportunity for these things to come up and develop.
>
> —Scott Stonehouse

Speaking of messages . . . do you know what I find confusing? A married person who does not wear a wedding ring. In my work I see many people who are serving in full-time ministry. On several occasions I have seen married guys without their rings on. Women notice that . . . and it sends a bad message.

"Eye Candy" Isn't Sweet

A friend of mine at work once told me he liked looking at women but his boundary only included looking. He playfully referred to attractive women as "eye candy."

His boundary is at odds with Jesus' words in Matthew 5: "But I say to you that everyone who looks at a woman with lust for her has already committed adultery with her in his heart" (v. 28 NASB).

In my life I have found that extended looks can quickly turn into lust. I follow the three-second-rule: I see her. She's pretty. Look away. Extended looks can be dangerous and you'll find that eye candy isn't healthy. So avoid it at all costs.

> While focusing on the sister/brother image, you are also erecting some barriers: no closed doors in offices, don't travel together as pairs, no rides home late at night, avoid personal issues or marital in-depth counseling. I would never talk to a woman about sexual issues with her husband, but I might talk about disciplining her children. It's about more conscious thinking: If my wife or husband walked in on what I'm doing, how would I feel? Would they be 100 percent fine with it? You can't really draw lines. It's about a commitment to purity—it's the air you breathe.
>
> —Dr. Andy McQuitty

Never Flirt Alone

We've all flirted with someone at one time or another. It starts in grade school and it never ends. After our marriage, however, we need to limit the number of people we flirt with down to one. I love flirting with my wife, but I know I would be on dangerous ground if I flirted with others.

I love laughing and having fun with people. When I say "never flirt alone," please don't take it as a green light to flirt so long as other people are around. Before I have playful fun with the opposite sex, I try to imagine how my wife would feel if she saw me (Ortberg's Screen Test). Would she laugh with me or would I hurt her feelings?

It's important to think of our spouse's feelings in our relationships with others.

Three's Company

After I had dinner with the ex-stripper, I made it a point to avoid opportunities to eat or travel alone with a woman. At work I have been to lunch with small groups of women, which works fine.

With men and women working together in the church and corporate America, this can sometimes be a real challenge. While some ministries do not allow men and women to travel together, it's another story in business. My best advice is to be very discerning and if you find yourself in a difficult situation, let your spouse and a friend know what your plans are. Under no circumstances would I entertain a meal or travel with someone who was a red alert for me.

> Here is my advice if you find yourself attracted to a coworker. Nip it in the bud in the early stages. Don't sit too close physically. Don't spend too much time together. If the issue develops, then seek counsel from a mature friend. The other "fence" is that you keep on task. The relationship is a professional relationship. What are you here to talk about? Not sexual issues, or problems with your wife or husband. You are here to talk about the task. Keep the relationship professional instead of personal. A discussion about anything intimate should always include more than one person,
>
> Dr Howard Hendricks

Complimenting Confusion

All of us enjoy compliments, but we need to be careful when we compliment the opposite sex. It's easy to be misinterpreted. Let's say a woman admires an article of clothing that a coworker is wearing.

It's one thing to say, "That's a nice shirt you are wearing." It's quite another thing to say, "You look good in that shirt." If you want to say something nice, limit the compliment to the item of clothing, not how they look in it. If someone is wearing something and it's obvious that it is new, it's OK to say, "Is that new? It looks nice."

With issues of performance, limit the compliment to the performance, not the person. It's fine to say, "Pastor, that was a great message Sunday." However, I would avoid comments like, "Pastor, you are an awesome speaker." Ortberg's Screen Test is effective here too. What would your spouse (or your coworker's spouse) say if they heard you say that?

Touching Trouble

In 1968, Jim Morrison and The Doors released a song called, "Touch Me," that went to number three on the billboard chart. It was a big hit for the group, but the chorus sends a bad message for fence builders. The singer pleads with a "babe" to touch him, and sexual overtones permeate the song.

There was a time when men and women were much more modest in their interaction with the opposite sex. When a man greeted a woman, both would extend their hands and it's quite possible that the woman wore a glove as she grabbed the man's hand loosely. How times have changed.

Touching can be taboo at work and in ministry. "The first—and most important—rule to remember is that beyond the handshake there are only three locations on the body where skin-to-skin contact is acceptable among coworkers: the forearm, the wrist, and the upper back," insists Jill Bremer, an image etiquette and communication skills instructor with Bremer Communications. "Longer than a couple of seconds and it can become sexual . . . remember to keep it light and fast. . . . Anything more and it makes the receiver wonder, what is this person trying to tell me?"[3]

A few months ago I spent time with two women I had just met, helping them with their work in ministry. We spent three hours together and, as we were saying our good-byes, I shook one's hand. As I extended my hand to the other woman, she reached in and gave me a big frontal hug.

She didn't mean anything by the hug. She was just appreciative of my help. In my fifteen years at Interstate Batteries, I can only remember hugging two women. I hugged one when I walked out of my office after getting the news that my brother had just died. I hugged the other when I attended the funeral of her father-in-law.

I know many women who hate it when guys hug them. I know other women who don't mind at all. The problem is that you can't tell them apart. Handshakes and side hugs are usually fine, but the discerning staff member will avoid frontal hugs.

I remember hearing a story about a pastor who would stand by the door and shake hands with the congregation as they left. One woman made it a point to hug him, and it made him very uncomfortable. He knew that 1 Corinthians 10:13 said that God will give us a way of escape when we are tempted, but in this situation he didn't see any escape. The following Sunday as the woman was walking down the aisle, he felt a pull on his pant leg. It was a child wanting his attention. He picked up the child and was only able to shake the woman's hand. He had found his way of escape.

I don't know if the cute story is true, but it reminds us that we need to look for ways of escape if someone gets too touchy. I have counseled a few people to simply say, "I'm uncomfortable when you do that." Speak truth with kindness. It works very well.

I have two primary fences. First, I must make my own marriage a priority. I find that a good marriage partnership is the best protection possible. Second, I maintain an open profession of faith. I always have found that my profession of faith sets a clear tone in all my relationships—with men and women. I try to set the bar high early on in my relationships and thereby hold myself accountable.

I am somewhat dubious of making rules, such as, keeping the door open when a female is in my office or never riding in a car alone with a woman. Some women find these rules insulting; it suggests to them that they are

> untrustworthy. Furthermore, these rules are impractical. Because I work with women leaders, I must have confidential conversations from time to time. Closing the office door for confidential discussions is a necessity in my job. I try to be prudent in all relationships, trust my instincts, and not do anything intentionally that would dishonor the Lord, my wife, or my fellow Christians.
>
> —Dr. Frank James

Well, you've read eight of my boundaries. All eight work very well for me and have helped me as I work with women. If you think the boundaries will work for you, then use them. Try to think of others that might work too. It would be a great exercise to talk to other peers and ask them what boundaries they use. One thing I know for sure: we all need boundaries.

Be on Guard

I'm a simple guy and I like guarding my heart. I love the NIV translation of Proverbs 4:23: "Above all else, guard your heart, for it is the wellspring of life." Solomon, the wisest man who ever lived, tells us that above all else, we are to guard our hearts. It's good counsel for us today.

In 1981, I was stationed at Fort Hood, Texas, as an infantry lieutenant. My battalion was sent to Fort Chaffee, Arkansas, to guard Cuban refugees. The refugees were either criminals or delinquent in some other way. They were kept in a compound with barbed wire fences. Outside the fence we had soldiers patrolling the perimeter. During the time my unit was deployed, we didn't have any refugees escape. The reason was simple. We were protecting the boundaries with great diligence.

And so it is with us who want to honor God with our lives. If we have no boundaries, or if we are not diligent about guarding our heart, we are bound to stumble. In fifty years of living, I have learned that it hurts to stumble. There is always a cost. Guard your heart.

Yes, men do find some women physically attractive. That's involuntary. But to men I say, what you are doing in your head is critical and you must deal with this yourself. You are responsible for what you do with that involuntary response. How do men protect themselves from infidelity? The answer is good sound mental health. We must ask ourselves, do I come to the table *without* emotional needs? If I do, it helps so much. And good sound mental health is critical for women too. If either one is emotionally needy, we have toxic problems. In ministry, we need emotionally mature men partnering with emotionally mature women.

Men need to ask themselves, "How do I feel when a woman praises me? Is this better than when men praise me? What if the woman is young? attractive?" If I need this attention, these are red flags that I am emotionally immature. I need to deal with this. And women need to ask similar questions.

The problem is that emotionally immature men are blind, and this is especially dangerous when the man is a pastor. When a woman in his congregation adores him, he thinks it is because he is adorable and his wife does not appreciate him. His wife has heard all his jokes and knows him too well. At home he is the "trashman" on the days the trash goes out—but not at church. If he is emotionally immature and needy, he is vulnerable to this unhealthy attention and he is in trouble.

An emotionally mature man will flush his mind with good thoughts about his wife. This is how I apply Philippians 4:8: "whatever is true, whatever is noble, whatever is right, whatever is pure, whatever is lovely, whatever is admirable—if anything is excellent or praiseworthy—think about such things." Years ago, I wrote down all the good things about my wife and bathed my mind in those good things. Now, years later, they come to mind naturally. I keep a healthy flow of positive thoughts in mind routinely. I don't criticize her and I don't let others criticize her either. I praise her publicly and this alerts needy women that I am spoken for.

Men are mistaken when they think that they cannot control themselves. We, as emotionally mature men and women, decide who we will release our emotions to—or not! This is a conscious choice. Men, if you are attracted to someone, you remind yourself of your wife, your children, what your life is about, and most of all your devotion to God. You are purposeful in every relationship.

If you are emotionally healthy, you can work with women. If you are not, you should not be in ministry. Work on your mental hygiene. Emotionally healthy men respond wisely to attractions. If you sense any kind of unhealthy attraction, you are careful and you create space. You keep your distance and you make sure the relationship does not move in an unhealthy direction. You may create physical space or you do not take as many appointments, and you do this because as a spiritual leader you are looking out for her welfare. You have her best interest at heart. You simply behave yourself and use good judgment.

And as ministry leaders, we are wise because we are "public" people. What we do impacts others and perception is critical. So I restrict my interaction with women to public places and I make sure my wife is aware when I am meeting with a woman. I make it a group as much as possible. I meet for breakfast or lunch but not dinner. That looks more professional. I never want to be in the position of having to explain what I did or what she did. When I travel, I don't travel alone with a woman or I make it a threesome. We must protect ourselves and always be above reproach. This is the Lord's church!

But this does not mean that I don't have women friends, and I enjoy a healthy emotional attachment to these women just like I would a sister or daughter. That relationship looks different than a relationship with men friends. I can talk about issues that we men have in common just as women share a special bond because of similar experiences and perspectives. But these relationships with women coworkers enrich my life.

—Dr. Michael Lawson

DISCUSSION QUESTIONS

1. Discuss John Ortberg's three tests.

2. Do you think it is wise or legalistic to construct protective fences? Explain your answer.

3. Consider the eight fences presented in this chapter. Would you add additional barriers? Would you tweak or eliminate any? Discuss.

4. Would any of these barriers be difficult to construct in your life and work? If so, why?

5. Have you experienced touching that seemed innocent but made you uncomfortable? How did you handle it?

6. How can we guard our hearts (Prov. 4:23) while continuing to create mixed-gender community?

7. To whom have you communicated your personal boundaries?

Chapter 14

Modesty: Exalting the New Taboo

Modesty is my best quality.

—JACK BENNY

Modesty? A source of great power? Yes. Modesty is the source of this delicate yet formidable power, making it a power in and of itself. It's delicate because it can be so innocently given away without you even knowing it. It's formidable—or difficult to deal with or control—because once you've mastered it, no man will be given access to the full secrets behind your allure until you so desire.

—DANNAH GRESH

DREAM WITH ME FOR A MOMENT . . .

Your suburban church begins growing rapidly. Every Sunday, more people crowd in. They lean against the back wall, crane their

---

Authors' note: You'll notice the tone and style of this chapter is different from the rest. We asked Eva Bleeker, our research and writing assistant for this book, to participate by writing this chapter since her ministry experience with young women has given her a passion for the topic.

necks to peek through lobby doors, some even come *early* to get a seat. Your leadership team decides to add multiple services to the weekend routine. But the Lord leads so many new people to worship with your congregation that your facility simply cannot hold them all. You pray for guidance and decide to build a larger space. Many of your new attendees come from the surrounding neighborhoods. They're young; many are single. You want to create an environment that makes them comfortable, that invites them in. You want to design something that makes sense to them. Finally the new worship center is ready. The front of the room—the platform—is not just for the pastor. This is a place for gathering. The stage is low, curving out in the middle toward the seats. A row of cushions laid on the floor follows the arc of the platform, a place to come and kneel. During each service, worshippers can come to the front, bow, kneel, pray, sing, even light candles. By the end of the service, the room flickers with reverence. You're thrilled. People are joining in this new style of worship—they're getting it! And more are coming all the time.

It's Sunday morning, and everyone in the worship center has just been led in beautiful music and prayer. Your pastor invites anyone present to participate in your church's unique and demonstrative act of worship, to come to the front. A woman in slinky jeans and a short blouse—maybe she's new, you haven't seen her before—climbs out of her row and plods down the aisle, slumped and crying. She is so overcome that two friends must support her arms and shoulders. She reaches the platform and kneels before the cross. And as she pours her heart out to Jesus, her blouse and jeans separate, baring much of her back and buttocks. Suddenly, in front of nearly a thousand people, this woman is undressed.

Now freeze. What are you thinking? Are you disgusted at this woman's lack of discretion? Are you men secretly bathing in lust? Are you pleased that she feels so drawn to Christ that she shows it by going forward? Maybe you have seen her before. Are you *sure* she's not one of your most devoted members? Hold that thought.

Cringing at Our Culture

Unquestionably, a lack of modesty dominates American culture. Things sure have changed! In its run from 1965 to 1970, NBC would not allow Barbara Eden's navel to be shown on *I Dream of Jeannie*.[1] Now, they just argue about what *time* the major networks can broadcast sex. You can read the details of nipple piercing, multiple orgasms, or the perfect Brazilian wax while you check out at Wal-Mart. Anyone still doubting the loss of modesty in America should ride the bus with elementary school students.

Or consider what happened to my husband, Josh, and me just this week. He had been out of town on a business trip, and we planned to celebrate his return by going out for dinner. We pulled into the parking lot of what we used to call "the fish place," but all the signs had changed. "Well, do you want to try this instead?" Josh asked. We got out of the car, and just as we rounded the building—the side of the restaurant with windows—Josh abruptly said, "Let's go." With his eyes trained on the sidewalk, he reversed his direction and headed back to the car. At the same moment, I got a good look at several of the servers through the windows. All of them were showing belly and legs; one was in full dominatrix gear. This is what their sign means by "scenic views."

In her book *A Return to Modesty*, Wendy Shalit describes the culture shift in the last few decades. American youth and young adults feel crushing pressure to look sexy. But the pressure goes beyond appearances. It used to be shameful to be sexually active. Now it is shameful to shun any kind of sexual activity. She explains that a preference for virginity or even sexual modesty is embarrassing, "as if admitting some depravity," and that "the objects of our shame have become so mixed up that modesty is now what is taboo."[2]

Of course there is nothing new under the sun. As we'll see later, the world of the apostles was not always G-rated. But Shalit's observations do represent a change in American society. I'm not one to harken back to the good old days, but not so long ago American girls felt much more resolve about developing their inward virtues than about looking great in a thong. Joan Jacobs Brumberg says that "when girls in the nineteenth century thought about ways to improve themselves, they almost always focused on their internal character and how it was reflected in outward behavior."[3] That perspective is exactly where we're going in this book.

Doing a Little Family Business

So, the country's mind is largely in the gutter. But if you're like me, you might be thinking, *Do we really have to have this conversation? Those of us who love Jesus? I mean Christian women should be bright enough to cover themselves at a worship gathering. And if Christian men are still aroused, they should be bright enough to look away.* Believe me, I have had this conversation. Many believing women defend their choices by citing their freedom in Christ, a concept I would defend zealously. Perhaps, though, we have failed to consider the consequences of exercising that freedom.

Our freedom must consider the dignity of others. That girl in the dominatrix outfit, just for a moment, preyed upon my husband's dignity. But even for those women trying to make good choices, it is difficult. I'm in my late twenties. What do I have to choose from at the mall? Clothing stores seem to have only two selections available: super-hoochie and extra-frumpy. My Christian sisters often choose the former.

Of course, things vary by region and from church to church. If your reaction to the story at the beginning of this chapter is shock and amazement—you just cannot imagine something so ghastly appearing in your sanctuary—consider the following scenarios. A male Christian counselor deliberately keeps the temperature in his office cooler than necessary to encourage women to cover themselves fully during counseling sessions. A young adult Sunday school teacher described a regularly attending woman in his class so inadequately covered that he was almost too distracted to complete the lesson—she was eight months pregnant and seated with her husband. A group of full-time church workers joked that the reason the lights are turned down during contemporary worship services is to conceal all the naked flesh in the room!

Recently, I spent a day shopping with two of my best friends. You would have trouble finding three more conservative girls. Our closets offer a selection of jeans, hiking boots, and ancient T-shirts. While pawing through sale racks at a trendy boutique-style store, we picked out things that we would never buy. Sassy, club attire has little place in a female seminarian's lifestyle. Or budget. "C'mon! Let's try these on," my girlfriend said, holding a strapless top. "It'll be fun." Oh, really? What makes it fun for three young women headed for career ministry to see themselves scantily clad? I suggest that many of us, my Christian sisters, have been seduced by the power of our own sensuality. Maybe, without even thinking about it, we have conformed to the patterns of this world. Or perhaps we are just like a New York City coed. When a minister explained that she was so valuable to God that she didn't need to attract men with her sexuality, that she was worth much more than that, she replied, "That's just too good to be true." If this is the state of things, what do we do?

Defining Terms

When we talk about modesty, what are we really saying? Most of our thoughts revolve around how we dress. And dress is part of it, but modesty is more than clothes. Even if we struggle to define modesty, we all sense when it has been violated. Remember your reaction when you pictured that young woman exposed in front of her congregation? James S. Spiegel helps us define terms, calling modesty "the moral skill of maintaining physical privacy and, in particular, exercising public restraint in the area of sensuality."[4] Spiegel says that while modesty differs from purity or chastity, "it overlaps with them. It is, one might say, the public expression of these traits."[5]

So modesty keeps some things secret while making other things very public. It hides the sensual parts of us and broadcasts inward values loud and clear. Modesty is an inside-out expression. But an expression of what exactly? Within the church, modesty should represent the sensual and sexual values of the Bible. So that means we only express ourselves sexually in marriage and in the bedroom.

The Scripture values modesty throughout its pages. On the flip side, Proverbs condemns attractive people (specifically women, I'm afraid) who flaunt what they've got. Their beauty is wasted; "like a gold ring in a pig's snout is a beautiful woman who shows no discretion" (Prov. 11:22). For five years, I lived across the road from a hog farm. Believe me, this is not a desirable category.

But speaking of the Bible, didn't God design people to run around naked in the first place? Why should it matter if we show a little skin now and then? Well, you might recall that within a few sentences of running around naked, things shifted globally for humankind. Nakedness was not the problem in the garden, but we're not in the garden. Both the apostle Paul and the apostle Peter gave us some great postgarden guidelines. First Timothy 2:9–10 and 1 Peter 3:3–5 encourage women to be attentive to modesty in their dress (the outside); by doing so, their Christlike character (the inside) will make them truly gorgeous. These passages emphasize the inside-out nature of true modesty. Plus Peter says that God is thrilled with this attitude.

> Your beauty should not come from outward adornment, such as braided hair and the wearing of gold jewelry and fine clothes. Instead, it should be that of your inner self, the unfading beauty of a gentle and quiet spirit, which is of great worth in God's sight. (1 Peter 3:3–4)

So What Do We Do?

I meant what I said before about our freedom in Christ. The church is not a place for specifics about hemlines and necklines, and I hope we don't invent a new kind of legalism for getting dressed. That wouldn't work anyway. Just as modesty originates on the inside, the standards of genuine modesty come from a spirit submitted to Christ. A list of rules would not fix anything. Also, prescriptions for dress tend to be limited to women, and modesty applies to men as well.

We all know men who operate out of their sexual charisma,

sparkling everywhere they go. Seldom does a man reveal too much skin in a worship setting, but demeanor is everything here. Besides, we all know men and women who manage to be provocative in a business suit. Instead, brothers and sisters, tackle your own hearts. Ask yourself this question: what is the point of my wardrobe? Do my clothes say, "I respect myself and you," or "Baby, there's more where this came from"? God graciously allows us to be naked without shame in marriage. But the reverse is true too; to suggest nakedness outside the husband-wife relationship *is* shameful. Let's take it a step further. What is the point of the way you walk, smile, or look at members of the opposite sex in the face?

A few comments from fellow seminary students illustrate my point:

> I would say to women who dress provocatively, it isn't *you* a man is lusting for, it is *your body*. You are incidental. You will not find a husband by dressing that way, and if you do he will not be a man you want to be married to. (male student)

> Women forget or don't realize how men are wired—we are stimulated visually. If you are single and want to attract a godly man—dress modestly. If you want to attract a man who struggles with the flesh and will be attracted to you for the wrong reasons, dress provocatively. (male student)

> Dressing provocatively? This is a real irritant for me! We want to be seen as godly women but we let it all "hang out" for all to see—clearly a disconnect! (female student)

> There are a large number of women who are more focused on their freedom in Christ than on the impact they are having on others with the way they dress. It may be lawful to dress in a certain way, but it may be to the detriment of others. (male student)

Christian modesty, the inside-out kind, allows us to represent the Lord God without compromising the dignity of those who see us. To do otherwise steals away dignity in a twinkling. I would implore you to consider these issues, in the privacy of your heart, as honestly as possible. Change—if you need to—where you need to. Not just your clothes but your objectives.

Thinking Fresh About Flesh

So, how do we foster a culture of modesty in our churches? I think the answer lies in taking this brother-sister thing seriously. You would never dress for a family dinner the way you would dress for a speed-dating party. And the church is a family reunion, celebrating Dad with the rest of the brothers and sisters. When we gather as believers, we come together as siblings in Christ.

It's amazing that I had any male friends growing up. In fact, my husband was the first guy ever brave enough to take me on a real date. Why? My guy friends were afraid of my father. He was never unkind to them. In high school, I lived just three blocks from school. Dozens of teenage boys tromped through our home, often stopping in the kitchen. Our church youth group gathered weekly in our living room. But despite the hospitality, many of them commented on their fear of my protective and rather gigantic dad. What if we thought about church this way? Our Father, hospitable and kind beyond belief, is honored by our modesty. What if we dressed for him rather than for each other? We would never provoke a sibling sexually. We honor God by implementing this thinking when we're at family reunions, and by remembering that we're part of that family all the time.

A Blessing in Disguise

If those of us who claim Christ began to shift toward inward and outward modesty, there could be great benefits for appropriate sexual relationships between Christian men and women. The following story by writer Naomi Wolf is an extreme example that communicates the incredible power of modesty.

I will never forget a visit I made to Ilana, an old friend who had become an Orthodox Jew in Jerusalem. When I saw her again, she had abandoned her jeans and T-shirts for long skirts and a head scarf. I could not get over it. Ilana has waist-length, wild and curly golden-blonde hair. "Can't I even see your hair?" I asked, trying to find my old friend in there. "No," she demurred quietly. "Only my husband," she said with a calm sexual confidence, "ever gets to see my hair."

When she showed me her little house in a settlement on a hill, and I saw the bedroom draped in Middle Eastern embroideries, that she shares only with her husband—the kids are not allowed—the sexual intensity in the air was archaic, overwhelming. It was private. It was a feeling of erotic intensity deeper than any I have ever picked up between secular couples in the liberated West. And I thought: Our husbands see naked women all day—in Times Square if not on the Net. Her husband never even sees another woman's hair.

She must feel, I thought, so hot.[6]

I repeat this story to preserve the idea that God is not horrified by our sensuality and sexual contact. Rather, it shows the power modesty holds to protect God's designs and boundaries for appropriate sensuality. Contrast this scene with the woman from the beginning of our chapter, inadvertently being sensual with a roomful of people. As Spiegel points out, "It seems that you can't lose with modesty. On the one hand, keeping one's bodily secrets naturally prevents unwanted and unhealthy sexual encounters, but by preserving an erotic sense of mystery it enhances one's sex appeal."[7] A paradox like that has to be a God thing.

Wrapping Up (Pun Intended!)

Before leaving this subject, let's review a few thoughts. Modesty is an inside-out attitude of reverence for Christ. Our inward devotion to him, which includes a wild respect for the dignity of all people, guides our choices. When any believer, male or female, suggests sexuality with clothing, body language, words, or anything else, we step outside God's boundaries for sex. We also compromise our ability to represent Christ by drawing the focus toward ourselves and away from him. Not to mention that we could lead a brother or sister to sin through lust, jealousy, or anger. That's the downside. The upside is that by prioritizing modesty, we can benefit from the abundant blessings of an appropriate, God-honoring relationship, and we are free to share Christ without the confusion of sex. Regarding each other as siblings helps us establish guidelines that are safe without being legalistic. Let's take this brother-sister thing seriously.

DISCUSSION QUESTIONS

1. Discuss the relationship between current fashion trends and modesty for the Christian.

2. Recall times when someone was immodest in your presence. How did you feel? What message would you like to send to immodest people?

3. Discuss the author's statement that modesty "hides the sensual parts of us and broadcasts inward values loud and clear."

4. Modesty is not just about clothes. What other attitudes and actions can be immodest?

5. Discuss the story by Naomi Wolf. Do you believe that James Spiegel is right that "preserving an erotic sense of mystery enhances one's sex appeal"?

6. Do you think all immodest people are aware of the way they influence others? Is it possible that you have been immodest yourself? How can Christians ensure that they are modest in their appearance, actions, and attitudes?

Chapter 15

Pornography

You wonder, "Am I doomed in my dilemma? I have left the door open for Satan, and he has taken advantage of my spiritual passivity. Can I get him out of the places he has wormed into?" The answer is a resounding yes! Jesus Christ is the Bondage Breaker.

—NEIL T. ANDERSON

IN 1959 HALL OF FAME COACH Vince Lombardi accepted the challenge to turn the Green Bay Packers franchise around. Legend has it that his first practice was quite interesting. Disturbed at what he saw on the field, he called for the players to come over and take a knee. He picked up the pigskin and said, "Let's start at the beginning. This is a football."

Well, men, as you consider working alongside women in ministry, can I (Henry) give you a news flash? Our thought lives concerning women can get us into trouble. Picture this moment. It's the bottom of the ninth in game seven of the World Series. The home team is down by three runs with two outs. The bases are loaded and up to the plate steps the home run king. As fans stand in anticipation, a woman two rows in front of you pulls off her top. Suddenly, the game no longer matters.

Guys, we're attracted to women and always have been. God wired us that way, but when we wrestle with pornography, we may fulfill our lust for a moment, but we will create problems in our lives that will cause us great harm.

I wish I could tell you that pornography has no impact on how men and women work together in ministry, but I can't. In 2001, *Leadership Journal* reported that 37 percent of pastors admitted that pornography was a struggle for them and 51 percent said it was a temptation.[1]

Men Who Fell

Over the past few years I have seen the devastating impact of porn with guys in ministry. Let me share two brief stories of men in ministry who fell:

- The leader of a missions organization went to a strip club and walked up to the stage to slip money into the G-string of a dancer. As their eyes met she covered herself and ran from the stage. She had been in one of the Bible studies he had taught.
- A church leader went to a club with a business client where one of the dancers recognized him. She had been a little girl on a soccer team he coached when his daughters were growing up. She, too, covered herself and ran from the stage.

You know what was interesting though? Neither of these dancers covered their faces. What they covered is what makes them different. And why did they run from the stage?

How many little girls grow up thinking, "When I get older, I want to be a doctor, lawyer, missionary, or a porn star"? Guys, healthy women don't choose to work in the porn industry. These women have to die emotionally to fulfill our lust. Each woman is someone's daughter! Can I ask you a question? How do want other guys to look at *your* daughter, *your* sister, *your* mother?

Do you see the problem? If you are one of those guys in ministry who struggles with pornography, know for certain that your porn habit will hinder your relationship with women colaborers for Christ. You won't see them through a brother's eyes. Lust and temptation will be a part of your relationship.

A Progressive Trap

Maybe you are reading this and saying, "Sure, I look at porn every once in a while, but I would never go into a strip club." Really? You may already know that pornography is progressive. It does not satisfy and it *always* leaves you wanting more. I have never met a guy who said, "When I was fourteen-years-old, I found a *Playboy* magazine, and that's all I look at today." Nope, I can't find that guy.

Several years ago I got a letter from an inmate who was arrested for going to a hotel room to have sex with two thirteen-year-old girls. In his letter he wrote, "Henry, I did something that day that five years earlier would have repulsed me." Yes, he had come to understand how progressive pornography becomes over time. And sadly, I know how progressive it is because of what I saw in my own life.

This chapter is from me, Henry, to you guys, man-to-man. I'm qualified to talk about it. I struggled with pornography as a child and young adult. I wrote a book about it, and I speak at men's retreats to help men understand that they can be victorious as we live in a sexually obsessed culture. Guys, you know by now the damage that porn is doing to men and their families. It's a growing problem with a devastating impact.

Pornography and the Internet

Let me give you some evidence. Anyone with a desire can buy an Internet domain for little money. I recently purchased one for $45 a year. One Web site recently sold for a bit more. Care to guess how much sex.com sold for? According to WebProNews.com, the sex site sold for a reported $12–14 million dollars.[2] You may be wondering why someone would pay that much money for a Web site. The answer is simple: they will get that money back and much more because Internet pornography has a huge following.

Consider the following statistics from the National Coalition for the Protection of Children and Families:

- 40 million Americans are sexually involved with the Internet.
- 70 percent of 18- to 24-year-old men visit pornographic sites in a typical month. 66 percent of men in their 20s and 30s also report being regular users of pornography.
- 25 percent of all search engine requests are pornography related.
- Sex is the number one topic searched on the Internet.
- 51 percent of U.S. adults surveyed believe that pornography raises men's expectation of how women should look and changes men's expectations of how women should behave.
- Americans spend $10 billion per year on pornography.[3]

Guys, the problem is impacting the pews and the pulpit. From involvement with pornography, we get a distorted view of sexuality and may find an increased risk of engaging in promiscuous behavior—*and* the behavior can even impact our relationship with female ministry workers.

Please don't think that you can compartmentalize porn. Maybe you have been deceived into thinking that you have your secret sin and that it does not impact your relationship with other women. That's one of the many lies porn wants you to believe.

So what do you do? We can't deny that we live in a sexually obsessed culture. Sticking our head in the sand won't work. We could refuse to work with women in ministry. Can I give you a better idea? It's pretty simple. Flee from sexual temptation. It seemed to work well for Joseph in Genesis 39. You know the story, but let's look at it again.

Joseph's Action Plan

In Genesis 39, Joseph was sold into slavery by his brothers and ended up in the home of Potiphar. He quickly earned the trust of his master who put Joseph in charge of everything he owned. Yes, Potiphar was pleased with Joseph, but so was his wife. When she gets Joseph alone, she says, "Lie with me." Was this a onetime offer? Hardly. In verse 10 we read that she spoke to Joseph *day after day*. Guys, there is one thing I know for sure . . . temptation once and temptation day after day are two different things.

Another aspect of this temptation is that no one would ever know. Who would find out? Would Joseph tell anyone? No, the cost was too great for him to be found out. Would Potiphar's wife say at an Egyptian bridge club meeting, "Ladies, guess who I'm having sex with behind my husband's back?" No, I don't think she'll be talking either. I can make a pretty good argument that this will be a secret for them both.

Well, what would you do if you knew for certain that you would not be found out? That's a test of character and Joseph passes with flying colors. His strategy? Flee. There's that word again. I love the first three words of verse 8. "But he refused." Guys, that's fleeing. Later in the story as she grabs his coat, Joseph actually runs from the room leaving his coat behind. He left his coat, but his character was intact. Joseph fled and so can we.

> Porn is the opposite of a brother-sister relationship. It's not about sex, it's about power and control. Men can't have power over other men so they make women the object of their attack. Recently, I was speaking at a Word of Life conference and it was a very conservative audience. Off the cuff in my message, I mentioned the dangers of pornography. Afterward six men came up and admitted, "You nailed me!"
>
> —Dr. Howard Hendricks

Paul's Advice

In his first letter to the church at Corinth, Paul wrote, "Flee sexual immorality! Every sin that a person commits is outside of the body, but the immoral person sins against his own body" (1 Cor. 6:18 NET). Involvement with pornography is a sin against our own bodies so Paul instructs us to flee. Guys, we would be wise to obey.

Paul does more than simply give us a command though. He tells us the "how" as well. Romans 13:14 says, "But put on the Lord Jesus Christ, and make no provision for the flesh in regard to its lusts" (NASB). OK, it seems that if we're not careful, we can make a provision for our flesh. Let me give you a few practical ideas on how to avoid doing so.

- Install blocking software on your computer.
- Place your home computer in a high-traffic area of the home with the screen facing the door.
- Avoid the newspaper inserts with lingerie ads.
- Have the movie channels disabled in your hotel room before you walk in the front door.
- Find an accountability partner that you trust with whom you can share your temptations and struggles.
- Cancel cable packages that offer pornographic movies.

Is there anything that you can add to the list? You may look at the list and wonder if it is really necessary. Yesterday I met with a man who does not struggle with pornography, but when he added cable to his home and saw what the options were, he asked his wife to have it disconnected the next day. Why? He knew it was time to flee. He was letting things into his home via the television set that he would not let in the front door.

A Wise Son

Years ago I stayed at a friend's lake house with my son. We had a great father-son weekend planned. When we were touring the house, we noticed a picture on the nightstand of this guy's wife in a very skimpy outfit. I left the room, but my son remained. When I went back a few minutes later, I noticed that the picture had been placed facedown.

I asked my son why he did that, and he replied, "Dad, we don't need to look at that." When I was his age I would not have put the picture down, I would have stolen it. I told my son that he has more

character at fourteen than I did at twenty-five. He understands
what it means to not make a provision. And he understands what it
means to flee.

The Cost

Can I give you the "rest of the story" as Paul Harvey would say?
Guys, there is a cost for our involvement in pornography. And the
cost is steep. I love asking guys to answer this question: *If I continue
to give in to sexual temptation, what are the consequences I may face in the future?* Grab a pen . . . take a minute . . . and make a list answering that
question. Guys, count the cost. I have a list that I keep in my Bible.
I have nineteen items on my list that I typed up and laminated. Let
me share a few items that are on my list:

- My wife, Kathy, would be devastated.
- I will grieve the heart of God who loves me.
- I will cause nonbelievers at work to see another hypocrite.
- It will affect how my children see their heavenly Father.

I periodically review my list and there is nothing on my list that
is an acceptable consequence for getting caught with pornography.
Why would I devastate my wife for the few moments of empty pleasure that sexual sin provides?

Another Important Reason

Can I give you one more to add to your list as you work with
women in ministry? I have already mentioned it once. Porn will influence how you see the women you work with. It is a privilege to
serve with our sisters in Christ, but our service will be hindered if
we have a problem with porn.

Many women do not knowingly provide temptations for guys,
but every once in a while, we may face an unexpected temptation. I
remember several years ago I had been asked to speak at a Campus
Crusade for Christ meeting at a university. My host was a delightful
woman named Traci whom God was using to make a huge impact

on campus. My wife was seated to my left and Traci was to my right. During the meal Traci dropped her fork on the floor and as she bent over, I knew her top would open. Do you know what she did? She placed her hand on the top to prevent it from opening. Whatever temptation I was facing was gone because of the kindness of my host. It's not that she thought I was a pervert, but she was being kind because she cared about me as a brother in Christ. I like that.

> We don't deny that sexuality between men and women in the workplace is an issue. What frightens us, however, and what I hear from pastors, staff, or female staff, is that of handling the potentials of harm by making sure that we don't really care for each other or know each other. The faulty assumption is that the more I know and care for you, the more potential there is for sexual violation. It is literally the opposite. The more distance, the more professionalism, the more presumption of boundaries actually creates a climate where power and eventually contempt have greater power. Most workplace sexuality isn't two people who have come to know each other inappropriately and then fall in love; most of it is power-based where a man with power is misusing a woman with less.
>
> —Dr. Dan Allender

Well, I can return the kindness by looking at her the way God wants me to see her. She is a crown of splendor, precious to our King! When guys struggle with porn, we don't see crowns of splendor; we see instruments of lust that feed our sinful desires.

Well, you know the good news! There is freedom in Christ. God's Word is true; he does indeed provide a way of escape when we face temptations. You will discover that when you are walking in victory, free from the power of porn, you will enjoy healthy relationships with women in ministry. Can you imagine what God will do with men and women who honor the King together? Do well, men.

DISCUSSION QUESTIONS

1. Enumerate the dangers of dabbling in pornography.
2. How does pornography influence our ability to see one another as spiritual brothers and sisters?
3. How can you protect yourself and your loved ones from Internet porn?
4. What is the role of the church in helping men and women gain victory over pornography?

Chapter 16

Safeguards for Spouses

*Marriage is like twirling a baton, turning handsprings, or eating with
chopsticks. It looks easy till you try it.*

—HELEN ROWLAND

*My wife's jealousy is getting ridiculous. The other day she looked at my
calendar and wanted to know who May was.*

—RODNEY DANGERFIELD

A True Story

Don carried the last box of belongings to his car, resolving never
to be in this situation again. Neither he nor his administrative assistant expected their relationship would turn into an emotional
affair, but it had. They both acknowledged the attraction before it
progressed too far, with Don taking primary responsibility. The senior pastor and elder board were gracious, as was his wife, Nicole.
Although deeply wounded, she forgave them both, but insisted on
marriage counseling. Don agreed, not only to counseling, but to immediate termination. Everyone conceded it was wise.

As Don thought back over these nightmarish three months, he
actually thanked God—in light of the possible consequences. "I
got off easy," he thought to himself. They were going home. Nicole

had been pressuring him to move back for years; her aging parents needed them. And an old classmate alerted him to a position that fit Don perfectly, executive pastor at a thriving church. Nicole was elated, as were their three girls and both sets of grandparents. Second chances.

Don showed up a half hour early the first day. Senior Pastor Nathan was already working on his sermon, but pushed back from his computer to greet his new recruit. Don had been honest with Nathan about the emotional affair, vowing that he had learned his lesson and would take proactive steps to protect himself.

Don plunged into his new position, working three or four nights a week and most weekends. Within six months both staff and congregation adored him. After each counseling session, Nicole was encouraged. They read the assigned books and talked through the exercises. But several months into therapy, Don told Nicole they didn't need to keep seeing the counselor. Besides, his schedule made it difficult to carve out time. He suggested that she go alone and she did twice, but it seemed futile to go without him. They settled into a routine, the kids adapted to school, and Mandy invited Nicole to join her leadership team.

For six years, Mandy, the women's minister, taught Bible studies and organized a flourishing ministry. Senior pastor Nathan and the elders, acting on a twang of guilt, hired her part-time, but her expertise, energy, and creativity soon bought her a full-time slot on staff, overseeing several ministries. Thirty-four and attractive, Mandy was happily married to Phil, a surgeon. In her former life, she partnered with men in the corporate world so the news that she would be working with Don on several projects did not bother her. But the news bothered Don, and it terrified Nicole. Unfortunately, Mandy reminded Nicole of Don's former administrative assistant—cute, competent, and outgoing.

Several weeks into their partnership, Don thanked God that he was not particularly attracted to Mandy, but he felt edgy around her anyway. In light of his previous failure, he evaluated everything they did through a sexual grid. He insisted she move her office farther away down the hall. When they both needed to attend a meeting off-site, he made a point of letting Mandy and everyone else know that he was not riding in the same car with her. He refused to sit near her at meetings and conversed by e-mail as much as possible.

Don and Nicole began sharing their testimony about all that "God did" to save their marriage, in every setting possible—Sunday school classes, at the elders' retreat, at youth meetings, with friends. Don prepared a seminar on ways to affair-proof your marriage, presenting it first to the elder board and then in a weekend format. In her small group, tearful Nicole constantly asked for prayer to protect their marriage. The issue became their identity.

One night after the women's leadership meeting, Nicole stayed behind. When Mandy asked how she could help, Nicole broke down sobbing. "Don cares more about what you think than about what I think. He never tells me what's going on—I just know this is not a healthy situation. I wish I understood more about ministry the way you do. I wish my opinions mattered more to Don. I wish I could figure out what God wants *me* to do with *my* life." Obviously Nicole was wounded, insecure, and jealous. Mandy prayed for Nicole, assuring her that she and Don were just friends, but Nicole abruptly stormed out.

Mandy was careful, dressing modestly, measuring every word and action. Wearied, one night she confessed to Phil, "Don's attitude toward me is handicapping my work. It's like he has introduced paranoia about the other sex into our church. I sense it everywhere I go, with other men who never looked at me like a sex object before. I just hope Don and Nicole can heal their relationship. More than anything, I want our working relationship to evolve beyond this." They invited Don and Nicole to their home for dinner, hoping to birth a friendship that might ease the tension. Don and Nicole declined. An icy silence clouded the staff and church.

A long year-and-a-half later, Nicole burst into the church office, tracked down Mandy and screamed, "I never see my husband and it's because of you! I just know there is something going on. You can't hide it anymore." Don and Nathan came running. They rushed Nicole off to Nathan's office, but she would not be soothed. Nathan suggested a counselor and Don said they would look into it. Everyone left rattled, with Don more than a little annoyed. For the next month, red-eyed Nicole cried through Sunday services and her small group.

There was "blood in the water" and word of the screaming incident circulated. The announcement said that Don decided to leave ministry and pursue a different dream. In reality, as he loaded the last box into his car this time, he had no idea what was next.

After they left, Nathan, Mandy, and the elders worked hard to overcome the climate Don and Nicole created—*women cannot be trusted to minister alongside men. It's a sex-saturated world and women are temptresses. It can only end in tragedy.* It had, but not for those reasons.

The staff and elders worked hard to restore a healthy climate and, in time, the church began to grow, but Mandy paid a high price. Some blamed her for Don and Nicole's departure. Mandy's ministry suffered, but, with Nathan's help, eventually the congregation welcomed her back.

■   ■   ■

This sad tale is true, although names and settings have been changed. What happened? Don sincerely desired to overcome sexual temptation in his life. But sexual temptation was not his core problem—at least not at Nathan's church. We applaud Don for confessing his emotional affair and taking steps to see that it did not happen again. But his efforts were misguided and he neglected the most important step. The real issue was his unhealthy relationship with his wife. Until they resolved the tensions in their relationship, "rules and regulations," throwing fits, or teaching seminars on the dangers of sexual temptations were smoke screens.

Don's refusal to see a counselor indicated that he was not willing to do the hard work required to build personal emotional health and a strong godly marriage. Nicole knew she was second fiddle to his work. Add his workaholic tendencies and the result was disaster. Several red flags waved to alert Don to the approaching crisis—Nicole's meltdown, Nathan's suggestions of counseling, Mandy's uptight attitude. But Don chose to wear blinders, costing him his ministry, marriage, and family.

Working as brothers and sisters involves additional relationships that we must consider. At home is a wife or husband who may eye this sibling friendship with suspicion: *Who is this person working side by side with my spouse? What is his or her intent? How close are they?* What can siblings do to ensure that spouses feel comfortable and that wise boundaries are in place?

Communicate Clearly and Frequently

Silence gives birth to outlandish imagination. Even secure spouses wrestle with jealousy when left in the dark. Talk to your spouse about your sibling partnership the way you would a same-sex friendship. Tell your spouse when you are meeting with a ministry sibling, and explain why. Be completely transparent. The Devil prowls around looking for a way to get into your spouse's mind with misinformation. Outsmart him by open communication. "I'm meeting with Sharon in the conference room this afternoon at 3:00 to decide how much to spend on our combined event. I just wanted you to know." Then when your wife or husband shows up at the office to find you meeting with a coworker of another gender, they won't be surprised. "Sharon and I are meeting with Betty Johnson this morning. She is going through a divorce and asked to meet with someone on staff. I included Sharon to have a woman present for Betty's sake." Without information, one day your wife or husband will find out and will want to know why you didn't tell them. So be kind. Put their mind and heart to rest. Be transparent.

It's especially important to disclose what's going on with a spouse who is unfamiliar with ministry. A "secret language" can marginalize the nonministry spouse. Some pastors keep silent under the guise of protecting their spouse, especially when there is conflict or personal attacks. Spouses may carry your offense, causing anger and pain, but if you include them, in the long run, they will feel involved in your life and work. Besides they are likely to find out anyway. It's far worse to hear the news through the grapevine and have to pretend that you know what's going on. Be sure "protecting" your spouse is not really an excuse. Communicating is hard work, especially when you've been talking all day. You may want your home to be a sanctuary from the tough issues of ministry. That's understandable, but this is not about you. It's about your spouse standing by you, praying for you, and feeling like a partner in your call—they can't if they don't know what's going on.

For a variety of reasons, spouses sometimes feel left out. Often they battle unrealistic expectations from the congregation. They hate "living in a fishbowl." In response they hide. A negative consequence is that they feel excluded. A minister who does not intentionally include his or her spouse makes that sense of isolation worse and may ultimately damage their marriage.

Ministers who tend toward workaholism should be even more intentional in keeping their spouses involved. If your life evolves around your church family, your spouse may feel like a stepchild, vying for attention and always coming in second. You are setting yourself up for trouble!

Our management team includes several women and several guys. We have management team retreats. When we started doing that, the first thing my wife wanted to know was, "What are the sleeping arrangements?" Her thoughts being, you're going to borrow someone's cottage and there's nine of you—how is this going to work? She had a valid question that was not driven by some kind of crippling fear—it was just a general wondering. How does this work with men and women who are leading a church, and doing a retreat together? The spouses have to be brought into the conversation as well so that everybody understands that we are aware of the issue, that great caution is going to be exercised, and that integrity is going to be insisted on across the board. But we are not going to be flaky about it and not allow church business to be done or the meetings to be held. We have work to do. So it has to be discussed and dealt with in wisdom.

—Bill Hybels[1]

Address the Issue of Attractions with Your Spouse

Attractions are normal—for both of you. Can you admit that to your spouse? Break the unhealthy silence. This is especially important for clergy because the average congregation is, on average, 60 percent female.[2] A pastor is around women all day and his wife knows it. Talking about the issue, sharing boundaries, and assuring her that you are careful will settle her heart.

We are not saying to tell your spouse every time you struggle with emotional or physical attraction, but openness to talking about the reality of attractions is helpful. After all, no one cares more for your purity than your spouse. You may ask them, "If I ever feel an attraction to someone I work with, how can I communicate that to you so that it encourages your prayer support and accountability without being threatening?"

For example, Pastor Tom and his wife, Janie, are open about their occasional attractions to someone at work. They don't feel betrayed because they understand that this is normal. As a result, they have promised to help each other through these instances. Janie knows the kinds of women that catch Tom's eye. Here is how they deal with sexual attractions to coworkers.

Tom doesn't have a problem with beautiful women. He likes perky women with lots of personality and wit. Once, Tom came home and asked me to attend a meeting with him that night. I asked why and he told me a certain woman would be there. I asked, if we were not married, would this be the kind of woman he would ask out, and he said yes. I knew he was struggling and needed my help. When I was younger, I would have been hurt. But that's silly. Everyone deals with this sometimes. I knew he was working on this in his head and heart and needed my help. It has happened to me too. I don't always feel the need to tell him, but I know I can if I need to. I tend to tell a dear friend and she prays with me and keeps me accountable. I went to the meeting with him that night, and told him I was praying for him. Later, he told me he didn't feel the pull anymore, but was being careful. And he told me how much he loved me and always wanted to be faithful to me. It strengthened our relationship.

We will all approach attractions differently, and we need the freedom to handle them with strategies that work for us. But consider creating an honest ethos between you and your spouse where you can help each other.

Get Help from Trusted Outside Parties

In our true-to-life account earlier, Mandy was open with her husband, Phil, who helped her cope with the tensions and confusion. On the other hand, Don was secretive with Nicole. We saw the consequences. But Mandy suggested another step that might have saved the situation. In hindsight, she admits that she should have gone to their boss and talked through the issues earlier. "Nathan, our senior pastor, was in the dark until it was too late. I wish all three of us had met to talk about appropriate boundaries and potential problems. It might have helped Don see how overboard some of his attitudes and actions were. Nathan was unaware of the issue until it boiled up."

Just like in a healthy family, we must face potential conflict before it reaches crisis stage. A third party might have helped Don work on the core problems instead of relying on obsessive fences to soothe his irrational fears and solve his problems at home. He paid a high price for refusing to continue therapy. A counselor, pastor, or wise friend can often see when we are blind. It's foolish to use calendars and cash to excuse an unwillingness to face personal problems, however agonizing. And bringing the spouses into the ongoing conversation might have saved everyone miserable heartaches—Don's job, his marriage, Mandy's reputation, and an unhealthy church ethos.

Seek Emotional Health Above Success

Success in ministry rests on our emotional health. When our lives are built on stability, honesty, integrity, and faithfulness, the Lord can use us to build thriving ministries that transform lives. Numerically, sometimes the fruit of our labor is large and sometimes small. It's up to the Lord. Our role is to walk close to Jesus, love others, work hard, and make wise choices.

Don had charisma, talent, gifts, and drive. But he was not willing to invest in his own emotional health or his relationship with his wife and family. Understanding ourselves can be the toughest work of all—but if we don't, we can't lead well or be trusted with the Lord's work. Don was not modeling Christlike character or obeying the commands of the Bible, which admonish us to put our loved ones above our own ambition. No matter how hard he worked to protect himself from sexual indiscretions, he missed the root cause and he destroyed himself, his ministry, and his family. His focus was on avoiding women as temptresses, rather than on nurturing his relationship with his wife. His plan backfired.

Become authentic men or women of God, bearing much spiritual fruit—and we won't find an affair waiting under every rock. The fruit of the Spirit— love, joy, peace, patience, kindness, goodness, gentleness, faithfulness, and self-control—will protect us from ourselves, others, and our enemy, the Devil.

When we can serve beside our brothers and sisters with integrity, with our spouses supporting us with confidence, it will greatly add to the health of our ministries and the glory of our Lord.

DISCUSSION QUESTIONS

1. Do you agree with the statement, "Attractions are normal"? Why do you think married couples tend to hide these attractions from their spouse?

2. How should a couple approach the issue of attractions outside the marriage? How much should a spouse disclose when he or she is feeling attracted to someone else? Would

you appreciate your spouse sharing this information with you? Why or why not?

3. Whom might you confide in when you struggle with an attraction outside of marriage?

4. Discuss communication skills that safeguard marriages.

5. How can we "seek emotional health above success"? Be specific and practical.

6. (For married persons to discuss privately.) Have you ever been jealous of your spouse's friendships at work, especially with someone of the opposite sex? If so, describe how you felt. How might your spouse have helped you overcome these feelings?

New Beginnings for Sacred Siblings

*Behold, how good and pleasant it is for brothers [and sisters]
to dwell together in unity.*
—HEBREW BOOK OF PSALMS (133:1)

*I urge you, brothers and sisters, by the name of our Lord Jesus Christ,
to agree together, to end your divisions, and to be united by the same
mind and purpose.*
—THE APOSTLE PAUL (1 COR. 1:10 NET)

THE E-MAIL FROM JANICE, our women's minister, read: "Can you join us for a meeting with the elders to discuss women in the church?" That's all we were told. Each woman cleared her calendar and showed up *early*.

Janice invited a smorgasbord of ten women. The former women's minister, now a Bible college professor, made the cut along with the pastor's wife and two lay leaders—one seasoned, the other new. Two "outsiders" received invitations as well. They worked deep within women's ministries at their churches and enjoyed a robust friendship with Janice. Two wide-eyed interns, both in their late twenties, hid behind nervous smiles as the men trickled in.

Five elders, the senior pastor, and the executive pastor greeted women they knew and introduced themselves to new faces. A buzz filled the room. Starbucks in Styrofoam cups. Chocolates unwrapped and savored. Men and women interspersed on leather couches and eclectic chairs, wondering.

Janice welcomed everyone on behalf of the elders and organized a "get-acquainted game" that required mixed-gender teams. *Enough fun—why are we here?* Janice then kicked off the conversation with an apology. "We did not tell you what to expect tonight because we did not want you to prepare anything. We just want to hear from you. Our church is wrestling with the issue of women's role in the church—and has been for some time. We want to create a policy. But first we want to hear from women about what it's like to be a woman ministering in the church today.

"Each of you brings something valuable to the discussion. Some of you carry a title and earn a paycheck. Others of you work as volunteers. Several of you, our women's ministry interns, are seminary students. And a special welcome to you two who don't attend our church but who can give us some insight into what's happening in other places."

Elder chairman George explained, "We guys were sitting around discussing the issue when suddenly it hit us—we are not women!" The room erupted in guffaws—the men pointing at each other in fun. "We don't know what it's like. So we asked Janice to help us out. And here we are. We *really* want to hear from you—no holds barred. Tell us what you say to each other behind closed doors. And what you say tonight stays in this room."

The women sat stunned. No man had ever asked them this question before. Silence. *Are these guys for real?* After more prompting, Carolyn, a lay leader, put her toe in the water. *Would the Red Sea part?*

I spent the last twenty years working alongside men as an executive vice president in the business world. You know the rules there. You work it out because the bottom line forces you to. Then I became a Christian and I still can't figure out the rules when it comes to my role as a woman. I find men less willing to take me seriously or even listen to me. It's been discouraging.

But I know that I want to serve Jesus. Two years ago I traveled to India on a mission team and the experience changed me. I want my life to count for eternity. In fact, I just resigned at work so I will be more free to serve the Lord. I'm not sure how it's going to play out but I know it's the right decision. But that doesn't mean I'm not afraid, especially when I think about working with men in the Christian world.

Several in the room encouraged her step of faith and listened attentively as she answered the elders' questions. Janice turned to the former women's minister, now a Bible college professor, "I bet Michelle has something to say." Michelle spoke softly at first, hands folded—gradually both voice and hands unfurled like a flag flapping in the wind.

Several years ago I explained to Jim [the executive pastor] that I was getting feedback from women visiting our church that obviously there was nothing for women here. Women like Carolyn came into our church and left saying, "It feels so male." This made me crazy because it isn't true. Women are valued and supported here, but you can't tell by attending a service. Men dominate everywhere—they greet, they usher, they do everything up front except sing. Jim listened and you know the changes. Women usher and greet now, but we still get similar feedback. Are there other ways to send the message that this church cares for women?

My women students wonder what their futures will look like. This afternoon I graded a paper by one of my brightest students. She told me that she almost dropped out of school.

Both she and her husband work and are pursuing degrees. They dream of serving God as missionaries: he as a church planter and she teaching women.

Their demanding schedule requires that her husband help with meals and housework, based on a plan they work out together. But when a woman in their church heard, she accused my student of not fulfilling her role as wife—"you are living in sin." Her counsel so shook my student that she contemplated quitting, even though she has only one semester to finish. Apparently my lecture on marriage roles freed her from this foolish action, and she was grateful, but still unsettled.

I find that Christian women today are terribly confused. They hear different voices—some encouraging them to pursue their gifts wholeheartedly and look for ways to serve Jesus. Others tell them that godly women stay in the shadows. If they follow their calling, they feel guilty. If they don't, they feel they are wasting their potential. Many women are sensitive, the messages go deep, and they latch on to varied voices that follow them through the years. They want to do what's right but they don't know what that is. For centuries, Christian women have been hearing different messages that continue to play in their heads.

Women nodded as Michelle spoke. The men listened and probed for details, without commentary. An intern went next.

My husband and I want to go on the mission field. We will finish seminary next year and we have contacted over twenty missionary agencies. Only two have shown any interest in including me as part of the team. My husband is adamant that we won't go with an agency that does not take me seriously. He has been shocked by their complete lack of concern over my character and credentials. He says, "It is like they don't see you or think you have anything to offer.

You have worked hard and your training is just as valuable as mine. I don't get it."

My husband calls the agency and the conversation usually goes something like this, "Yes, we would love to look over your resume and consider you for our team. No, we don't need to see anything from your wife." We have signed on with one of the two agencies that wanted to interview me too. But the whole process has made me feel like a non-person. It has really upset my husband.

Darlene, one of the guests, told her story.

I'm the first director of women's ministries and the only woman on staff at our church. It was a big step for the elders to hire me. I love my work but most of the men on staff don't know how to include me. I'm ignored at staff meetings and not invited to staff retreats. Most of you have heard by now that our senior pastor has resigned, left his family, and taken off with a single woman half his age whom he was counseling. We are devastated and wounded. But the incident seems to have made it worse for women. It's like we are the enemy, like we have leprosy. I don't know if our church will ever recover and I don't know if the men will ever accept me as a valuable player on the team.

The other guest, Cynthia, described her relationship with the male staff at her church.

I speak up at staff meetings and the men listen but seldom take me seriously. Our pastor is preaching a series on the Ten Commandments, entitled "Man Law." He uses those funny beer commercials to add humor to the message each week, and the men love it. But the women, well, let's just say, it doesn't work for them. I give men feedback from women each week in staff meeting and they just laugh at me. I love serving with these men but I often feel trivialized, like I'm not even there.

Hostess Janice jumped in.

I used to feel that way in the early days when there were only a few women on staff but now that there are more of us, it's much better. And our executive pastor has worked hard to give everyone a place at the table. We've even had conversations about the different ways men and women interact at meetings and how to set a tone where everyone is respected and contributes. I do feel valued although I sometimes hesitate to say much. But that's *my* problem, and not anything the men have done. I'm making progress because I know the men care for me and want my ministry to thrive. And I know our church benefits from the input of the women leaders.

Conversation continued for several hours, women venting and commending, men listening and commenting occasionally. At the promised time, Elder George ended the discussion, thanking everyone for their honesty. "This has been eye-opening to say the least," he added. "The time you invested tonight will help us create a policy, and I know one thing that has changed for me. This issue isn't just theoretical—now, it's personal." The other men nodded, pensive as if awakened to a new reality.

Several stayed behind for private conversations or to explore follow-up questions. Finally, Janice turned out the lights and walked a group of women to the exit. Usually talkative, now silent. They parted into the night, demure smiles on their lips and springs in their steps. New beginnings as sisters and brothers in Christ. New hope for his kingdom.

DISCUSSION QUESTIONS

1. What do you think a mixed-gender gathering with your church leadership would look like?
2. Which chapter has influenced you the most? Which chapter changed your thinking about the sacred sibling relationship?
3. If you had a second copy of this book, whom would you give it to? Who needs to wrestle with this issue?
4. What commitments are you willing to make as a result of reading this book?

Notes

Chapter 1: New Eyes

Epigraph. "We Will Stand," words and music by Russ Taff, Tori Taff, and James Hollihan (Word Music, 1983).

1. *When Harry Met Sally*, starring Billy Crystal and Meg Ryan, directed by Rob Reiner, written by Nora Ephron (Los Angeles: MGM, 1989).

2. Ibid.

3. I Am Next, "People," http://www.iamnext.com/people/911heroes .html.

4. See Kristen Talbot's story at the National Speedskating Museum and Hall of Fame at http://www.nationalspeedskatingmuseum.org.

5. Paul Gray and Lynda Manning, interview by Lesa Engelthaler, summer 2006.

6. Joye Baker, "An Analysis of the Leadership Challenges Facing the Dallas Theological Seminary Women Alumnae" (D.Min. diss., Dallas Theological Seminary, 2004).

7. Dr. John Ortberg (M.Div., Ph.D., Fuller Seminary) is senior pastor at Menlo Park Presbyterian Church in Menlo Park, California.

8. Benton Johnson, Dean Hoge, and Donald Luidens, "Mainline Churches: The Real Reason for Decline," *First Things* 31 (March 1993): 13–18.

9.   George Barna, "One in Three Adults Is Unchurched," *The Barna Update*, March 28, 2005, 1. This article can be found online at http://www.barna.org/FlexPage.aspx?Page=BarnaUpdate& BarnaUpdateID=185.

10.   George Barna, "Women Are the Backbone of the Christian Congregations in America," *The Barna Update*, March 6, 2000, 4. This article can be found online at http://www.barna.org/FlexPage.aspx ?Page=BarnaUpdate&BarnaUpdateID=47.

11.   See Wayde Goodall, *Why Great Men Fall: 15 Winning Strategies to Rise Above It All* (Green Forest, AR: New Leaf Publishing, 2005), 56–60; and John W. Thoburn and Jack O. Balswick, "Demographic Data on Extra-Marital Sexual Behavior in the Ministry," *Pastoral Psychology* 46, no. 6 (1998): 447–57.

12.   Jay Quine (president, College of Biblical Studies, Houston, Texas), in interview by authors.

13.   Jim Thames (associate professor of Christian education; associate academic dean, Academic Administration; director, External Studies, Dallas Theological Seminary, Dallas, Texas), in interview by authors.

Chapter 2: Not Segregation but Transformation

      Epigraph. Stuart Hample and Eric Marshall, compilers, *Children's Letters to God: The New Collection* (New York: Workman Publishing, 1991), n.p.

1.   The entire account is found in John 11:1–44.

2.   Mark Bailey, chapel message at Dallas Theological Seminary, Dallas, Texas, March 2007.

3.   Ben Witherington III, *Women in the Ministry of Jesus: A Study of Jesus' Attitudes to Women and Their Roles as Reflected in His Earthly Life* (New York: Cambridge University Press, 1987), 9.

4.   Loren Cunningham and David Joel Hamilton, *Why Not Women? A Fresh Look on Women in Missions, Ministry, and Leadership* (Seattle: YWAM Publishing, 2000), 64.

5.   Letter to author Sue Edwards, February 2007. Used by permission. Names changed to protect anonymity.

6. John Gray, in his best-seller, *Men Are from Mars, Women Are from Venus: The Classic Guide to Understanding the Opposite Sex* (New York: HarperCollins, 1992), described men and women as so different that they could have come from different planets.

7. Carolyn Custis James, *When Life and Beliefs Collide* (Grand Rapids: Zondervan, 2001), 176.

8. We discover her identity in the parallel passage of John 12:1–8.

9. Philip Yancey, *What's So Amazing About Grace?* (Grand Rapids: Zondervan, 1997), 26.

10. Bill Hybels is the founding and senior pastor of Willow Creek Community Church, and is well known for his relevant, insightful Bible teaching. He is the author of seventeen books and serves as chairman of the Willow Creek Association's board of directors. His quotes are taken from "Defining Moments: Women in Leadership," audio discussion, Willow Creek Association, 2004.

Chapter 3: Paul—a Brother?

Epigraph. Stuart Hample and Eric Marshall, compilers, *Children's Letters to God: The New Collection* (New York: Workman Publishing, 1991), n.p.

1. The Samaritan woman (John 4:1–26), the woman caught in adultery (John 8:2–11), and the woman who bathes Jesus' feet with her tears (Luke 7:36–50).

2. George Barna, "Women Are the Backbone of the Christian Congregations in America," *The Barna Update*, March 6, 2000. This article can be found online at http://www.barna.org/FlexPage.aspx?Page=BarnaUpdate&BarnaUpdateID=47.

3. Elaine Pagels, *Beyond Belief: The Secret Gospel of Thomas* (New York: Random House, 2003).

4. Dan Brown, *The Da Vinci Code: A Novel* (New York: Doubleday, 2003).

5. Judith Evans Grubbs, *Women and the Law in the Roman Empire: A Sourcebook on Marriage, Divorce and Widowhood* (New York: Routledge, 2002), 60.

6. Margaret Y. MacDonald, "Reading Real Women Through the Undisputed Letters of Paul," in *Women and Christian Origins*, ed. Ross

Shepard Kraemer and Mary Rose D'Angelo (New York: Oxford University Press, 1999), 207.

7. See Mark 10:43; Romans 13:4; 15:8; 1 Corinthians 3:5; 2 Corinthians 3:6; 6:4; 11:15; Galatians 2:17; Ephesians 6:21; Colossians 1:7, 23, 25; 1 Thessalonians 3:2; 1 Timothy 4:6.

8. John Witmer, "Romans," in *The Bible Knowledge Commentary: New Testament, An Exposition of the Scriptures by Dallas Seminary Faculty*, ed. John F. Walvoord and Roy B. Zuck (Wheaton, IL: Victor Books, 1983), 499.

9. "Prostates," in *The Zondervan Parallel New Testament in Greek and English* (Grand Rapids: Zondervan, 1975), 481.

10. Sir James Donaldson, *Woman: Her Position and Influence in Ancient Greece and Rome* (Whitefish, MT: Kessinger Publishing, 2005), 87.

11. Stanley Toussaint, "Acts," in *Bible Knowledge Commentary*, 405.

12. Barna, "Women Are the Backbone."

13. Was Junia a man or a woman? The name can be either masculine or feminine, so no one knows, although many argue fervently for their advantage. If Junia was a woman, she was a female apostle, messing up some scholars' categories. John Witmer speculates that Andronicus and Junia may have been husband and wife or that Paul may be using the term apostle in a broader, general sense, the way in which Barnabas, Silas, and others were called apostles, but not part of the original Twelve. ("Romans," in *Bible Knowledge Commentary*, 499–500.) Whether male or female, Junia was a respected believer who had come to faith before Paul and enjoyed a well-earned reputation for a lifetime of service and devotion to God. More than that no one can be sure.

14. Witmer, "Romans," in *Bible Knowledge Commentary*, 399.

15. Bruce W. Winter, *Roman Wives, Roman Widows: The Appearance of New Women and the Pauline Communities* (Grand Rapids: Eerdmans, 2003), 141ff.

16. Paul's letter to the Philippians reflects their tender relationship. See 4:14 to learn of their generous financial gifts.

17. W. E. Vine, "aged," in *An Expository Dictionary of New Testament Words* (Old Tappan, NJ: Revell, 1966), 1:43.

18. Vine, "new," in *Expository Dictionary*, 3:110.

19. Michael Grant, *The World of Rome* (London: Phoenix Press, 2000), 72.

20. Vine, "teacher," in *Expository Dictionary*, 4:112.

21. Vine, "sober," in *Expository Dictionary*, 4:44.

22. U.S. Census Bureau, 2000 Census, http://www.census.gov/population/socdemo/gender/ppl-121/tab02.txt.

23. U.S. Census Bureau, 2000 Census, http://www.census.gov/population/socdemo/gender/ppl-121/tab09.txt.

24. Loren Cunningham and David Joel Hamilton, *Why Not Women? A Fresh Look on Women in Missions, Ministry, and Leadership* (Seattle: YWAM Publishing, 2000), 232.

Chapter 4: It's a Family Thing

Epigraph. Garrison Keillor, quoted in "Brainy Quote," http://www.brainyquote.com/quotes/authors/g/garrison_keillor.html.

Epigraph. Pamela Dugdale, quoted in "Quote Garden: Quotations About Sisters," http://www.quotegarden.com/sisters.html.

1. Sarah Sumner, *Men and Women in the Church* (Downers Grove, IL: InterVarsity Press, 2003), 304.

2. While incest has certainly been practiced in various cultures throughout history, it has never been accepted as the model for sexual relationships. In America it is considered rape, child abuse, and a criminal act. More information can be found at, among other places, the National Center for Victims of Crime at http://www.ncvc.org/ncvc/main.aspx?dbName=DocumentViewer&DocumentID=32360.

3. Other scriptural commands against incest are Leviticus 18:6–18; 20:11–21; Deuteronomy 22:30; 27:16, 20, 22–23.

4. "By birth or law" refers to families connected by genetics and those joined by adoption.

5. Sumner, *Men and Women in the Church*, 304.

6. Jeffrey Kluger, "The New Science of Siblings," *Time Magazine* 168, no. 2 (July 10, 2006): 47–55. Also available online at http://www.time.com/time/magazine/article/0,9171,1209949-1,00.html.

7. Personal e-mail to Sue Edwards from Mark Heinemann, spring 2007.
8. Kluger, "New Science of Siblings," 55.
9. Feedback from evaluations at Dallas Theological Seminary, Dr. Sue Edwards, fall 2006.
10. Ibid.
11. Kluger, "New Science of Siblings," 54.
12. John Steinbeck, *East of Eden* (New York: Penguin Books, 1952), 267.
13. Midwest Adoption Center, "Sibling Rivalry," http://www.macadopt .org/MACSite%20Folder/articles.htm#Part1.

Chapter 5: Creating a Family Ethos for Brothers and Sisters

Epigraph. Amy Carmichael, *If* (Ft. Washington, PA: Christian Literature Crusade, 1992), 82.

1. For a thorough discussion, see preface to the NET Bible at http:// www.bible.org/netbible/pre.htm.
2. Dan Allender, *Leading with a Limp* (Colorado Springs: Waterbrook, 2006), 115.
3. Ibid., 116.
4. A phrase from Howard Hendricks, distinguished professor and chair of the Center for Christian Leadership, Dallas Theological Seminary. This is also a direct quote taken from David A. Peoples, *Presentations Plus: David Peoples' Proven Techniques*, 2nd ed. (New York: John Wiley & Sons, 1992), 29.
5. Michael Philip Penn, *Kissing Christians: Ritual and Community in the Late Ancient Church* (Philadelphia: University of Pennsylvania Press, 2005), 13. He says, "Friends also frequently kissed each other. There are dozens of references to male friends kissing, a few to female friends, and one to a male and female friend exchanging a kiss. Particularly common was a public greeting kiss and a kiss before departing. These too mainly occurred on the lips. Among Jewish sources, however, most kisses were on the head, hand, or feet."
6. Elizabeth Hill, Terry O'Sullivan, and Catherine O'Sullivan, *Creative Arts Marketing*, 2nd ed. (New York: Butterworth Heinemann,

2003), 293. "For those new to the building, Tate identified that they needed to establish a relationship with the visitor as soon as they walked in, making them feel welcome." Also see Wanda Vassallo, *Church Communications Handbook: A Complete Guide to Developing a Strategy, Using Technology, Writing Effectively, Reaching the Unchurched* (Grand Rapids: Kregel, 1998), 46–56.

7. Haddon Robinson, *Our Daily Bread*, Radio Bible Class Ministries, July 2006, July 30 entry.

8. Stanley Toussaint, "Acts," in *The Bible Knowledge Commentary: New Testament, An Exposition of the Scriptures by Dallas Seminary Faculty*, ed. John F. Walvoord and Roy B. Zuck (Wheaton, IL: Victor Books, 1983), 387.

9. Ibid.

Chapter 6: Brothers and Sisters: The Same, Only Different

Epigraph. Ann Spangler and Shari MacDonald, eds., *Don't Stop Laughing Now! Stories to Tickle Your Funny Bone and Strengthen Your Faith* (Grand Rapids: Zondervan, 2002), 28.

1. M. Gay Hubbard, *Women: The Misunderstood Majority*, Contemporary Christian Counseling, ed. Gary R. Collins (Waco, TX: Word, 1992), 98–99.

2. Ibid., 99–100.

3. Ibid., 117.

4. Dan B. Allender and Tremper Longman III, *Intimate Allies* (Wheaton, IL: Tyndale House, 1995), 19.

5. Tertullian, *De Cultu Feminarum* 1.1.

6. Augustine, *The Catechetical Instruction*, trans. Joseph P. Christopher (Westminster, MD: Newman Press, 1952), 18:29, 58.

7. Will Durant, *The Reformation: A History of European Civilization from Wycliffe to Calvin, 1300–1564, and Other Leaders of Protestant Thought* (New York: Simon and Schuster, 1957), 416.

8. Joan Jacobs Brumberg, *The Body Project: An Intimate History of American Girls* (New York: Vintage Books, 1998), 7–11.

9. Flora Davis, *Moving the Mountain: The Women's Movement in America Since 1960* (Champaign, IL: University of Illinois Press, 1999), 475.

10. *The Simpsons*, episode 375, first broadcast April 30, 2006, by FOX, directed by Nancy Kruse and written by Matt Selman.
11. Doreen Kimura, *Sex and Cognition* (Cambridge, MA: MIT Press, 2000), 3.
12. Leonard Sax, *Why Gender Matters* (New York: Broadway Books, 2005), 6–7.
13. Herbert Lansdell, "Sex Differences in Hemispheric Asymmetries of the Human Brain," *Nature* 203 (August 1, 1964): 550.
14. Paul Julius Möbius, *Ueber den physiologischen Schwachsinn des Weibes* (Halle, Germany: n.p., 1901).
15. Sax, *Why Gender Matters*, 31–32.
16. Ibid., 12–15.
17. Ibid., 32.
18. This conclusion is drawn from three studies: (1) Barbara Cone-Wesson and Glendy Ramirez, "Hearing Sensitivity in Newborns Estimated from ABRs to Bone-Conducted Sounds," *Journal of the American Academy of Audiology* 8 (1997): 299–307; (2) Yvonne Sininger, Barbara Cone-Wesson, and Carolina Abdala, "Gender Distinctions and Lateral Asymmetry in the Low-Level Auditory Brainstem Response of the Human Neonate," *Hearing Research* 126 (1998): 58–66; and (3) Giuseppe Chiarenza, Giulia D'Ambrosio, Adriana Cazzullo, "Sex and Ear Differences of Brain-Stem Acoustic Evoked Potentials in a Sample of Normal Full-Term Newborns," *Electroencephalography and Clinical Neurophysiology* 71 (1988): 357–66.
19. Jennifer Connellan et al., "Sex Differences in Human Neonatal Social Perception," *Infant Behavior and Development* 23 (2000): 113–18. See also Claire Meissirel et al., "Early Divergence of Magnocellular and Parvocellular Subsystems in the Embryonic Primate Visual System," *Proceedings of the National Academy of Sciences* 94 (1997): 5900–5905.
20. Georg Gron and Matthias Riepe, "Brain Activation During Human Navigation: Gender-Different Neural Networks as Substrate of Performance," *Nature Neuroscience* 3 (2000): 404–8.

21. William Killgore, Mika Oki, and Deborah Yurgelun-Todd, "Sex-Specific Developmental Changes in Amygdala Responses to Affective Faces," *NeuroReport* 12 (2001): 427–33.
22. Lizette Peterson, Tammy Brazeal, Krista Oliver, and Cathy Bull, "Gender and Developmental Patterns of Affect, Belief, and Behavior in Simulated Injury Events," *Journal of Applied Developmental Psychology* 18 (1997): 531–46.
23. Janet Lever, "Sex Differences in the Games Children Play," *Social Problems* 23 (1976): 478–87.
24. Kimura, *Sex and Cognition*, 68.
25. Carol Gilligan, *In a Different Voice* (Cambridge, MA: Harvard University Press, 1982), 64–105.
26. "God blessed them and said to them, 'Be fruitful and increase in number; fill the earth and subdue it. Rule over the fish of the sea and the birds of the air and over every living creature that moves on the ground'" (Gen. 1:28).
27. Both responses reflect the character of God. "The Lord passed by before him and proclaimed: 'The Lord, the Lord, the compassionate and gracious God, slow to anger, and abounding in loyal love and faithfulness, keeping loyal love for thousands, forgiving iniquity and transgression and sin. But he by no means leaves the guilty unpunished . . .'" (Exod. 34:6–7 NET).
28. Dan Allender, *Leading with a Limp* (Colorado Springs: Waterbrook, 2006), 121.

Chapter 7: For Sisters' Eyes Only

Epigraph. Bernard Rodgers and Nile Rodgers, composers, "We Are Family," performed by Sister Sledge in 1979.
1. George Barna, "Women Are the Backbone of the Christian Congregations in America," *The Barna Update*, March 6, 2000. This article can be found online at http://www.barna.org/FlexPage.aspx?Page=BarnaUpdate&BarnaUpdateID=47.
2. Linda Babcock and Sara Laschever, *Women Don't Ask: Negotiation and the Gender Divide* (Princeton, NJ: Princeton University Press, 2003), 1.

3. Max Lucado, *Next Door Savior* (Nashville: Thomas Nelson, 2003), 29–31.

4. John D. Grassmick, "Mark," in *The Bible Knowledge Commentary: New Testament, An Exposition of the Scriptures by Dallas Seminary Faculty*, ed. John F. Walvoord and Roy B. Zuck (Wheaton, IL: Victor Books, 1983), 135.

5. Ibid.

6. Leonard Sax, *Why Gender Matters* (New York: Broadway Books, 2005), 45–46.

Chapter 8: For Brothers' Eyes Only

Epigraph. William P. Merrill, "Rise Up, O Men of God," music by Aaron Williams, 1911.

1. Charlotte Whitton, quoted in "Wisdom Quotes: Quotations to Inspire and Challenge," http://www.wisdomquotes.com/001554.html.

2. George Santayana, quoted in George Whitton, *Persons and Places: The Middle Span* (n.p., 1945).

3. Michael Lawson, personal interview with authors, spring 2006.

4. Howard Hendricks, personal interview with authors, spring 2006.

5. Michael Lawson, personal interview with authors, spring 2006.

6. Howard Hendricks, personal interview with authors, spring 2006.

7. Bill Hybels, "Defining Moments: Women in Leadership," audio discussion, Willow Creek Association, 2004.

8. Steve Roese, personal interview with authors, September 5, 2006.

9. John Ortberg, personal e-mail to authors, summer 2006.

Chapter 9: The Elephant in the Family Room

Epigraph. Desmond Tutu, *God Has a Dream: A Vision of Hope for Our Time* (New York: Doubleday, 2004), 22.

1. George Barna, "Women Are the Backbone of the Christian Congregations in America," *The Barna Update*, March 6, 2000, 1. This

article can be found online at http://www.barna.org/FlexPage.aspx
?Page=BarnaUpdate&BarnaUpdateID=47.

2. Tertullian, *De Cultu Feminarum* 1.1.

3. Arthur F. Ide, *Woman: A Synopsis*, vol. A of From the Dawn of Time
to the Renaissance (Mesquite, TX: Ide House, 1983), 93–94.

4. Eusebius, *History of the Church* 6.8.

5. Dave Roberts, *Following Jesus: A Non-Religious Guidebook for the Spiritually Hungry* (Orlando, FL: Relevant Books, 2004), 165. Pharisees
are also compared to the Taliban in Brian R. Farmer, *American Con-
servativism: History, Theory, and Practice* (Newcastle, U.K.: Cambridge
Scholars Press, 2005), 53.

Chapter 10: New Lighting in the Church

Epigraph. Dio Chrysostom, eleventh discourse, chapter 2, quoted
in John Bartlett, *The Shorter Bartlett's Familiar Quotations* (New York:
Pocket Books, 1953), 74.

1. *Everything Is Illuminated*, a 2005 film by Warner Independent Pictures based on a novel of the same name by Jonathan Safran Foer,
Everything Is Illuminated (New York: Harper Perennial, 2005).

2. Aaron D. Davis, *Love Thy Neighbor . . . ? When a Spirit of Religion Opposes
the Heart of God* (Bloomington, IN: AuthorHouse, 2005), 76–77.

3. Anonymous, "The War Within Continues: An Update on a
Christian Leader's Struggle with Lust, Part 2" *Leadership* 9, no.
1 (1988): 24. This article can be found online at http://www
.christianitytoday.com/le/classics/war2.html.

4. Scott Winn, "Lust and Pornography—The Great Exchange: Trading
the Truth for a Lie," Richland Bible Fellowship, Richardson,
TX, August 27, 2006. This sermon can be heard at http://www
.podcastdirectory.com/podshows/744968. Pastors and teachers
considering a series on sex might benefit from reading Bryan
Wilkerson's article "The Joy of Preaching Sex," *Leadership Journal*
27, no. 1 (Winter 2006): 44–49.

5. J. Lee Jagers, *Hem of Christ's Garment*, audio file, Dallas Theological
Seminary, September 12, 2006, available at http://boss.streamos
.com/download/dts/feeds/chapel/mp3/20060912.mp3.

Chapter 11: Jesus and Wild Women

 Epigraph. Stuart Hample and Eric Marshall, composers, *Children's Letters to God* (New York: Workman Publishing, 1991), n.p.

1. James Reed and Ronnie Prevost, *A History of Christian Education* (Nashville: Broadman & Holman, 1998), 102.

2. "New Testament scholars debate whether this story belongs where it is in John, but others who think not also argue it probably is an authentic Jesus story." Darrell Bock, research professor in New Testament studies, Dallas Theological Seminary, in a personal e-mail to Sue Edwards, August 25, 2006.

3. Ms. Kimberly Lawson, a Young Life staff member at the time, shared these thoughts with her discipleship group of young girls in 1994. We picked up her insights from her father, Dr. Michael Lawson, who shares them whenever he teaches the gospel of John.

4. See http://www.magdelene.org for historical background on how the church interpreted John 8:2–11 and related passages.

5. Dr. Eugene Peterson is the professor emeritus of spiritual theology at Regent College in Vancouver, British Columbia. He is the author of numerous books, most notably *The Message*, his translation of the Bible. This quote was taken from an interview with Sandra Glahn in Glyn Erie, CO, 1996.

6. Philip Yancey, *What's So Amazing About Grace?* (Grand Rapids: Zondervan, 1997), 11.

7. Ibid.

Chapter 12: Color-Coded Attractions

 Epigraph. Hindu proverb, quoted in Jack Canfield, *Chicken Soup for the Single Parent's Soul* (Deerfield Beach, FL: HCI, 2005), 27.

1. Scott Stonehouse in an interview with Lesa Engelthaler on August 16, 2006.

2. Some helpful ministries include Focus on the Family, 800-A-FAMILY (800-232-6459); American Family Association, 662-884-5036; National Coalition for the Protection of Children and Families, 513-521–6227; Pure Online, 888-580-PURE; and Pure Life Ministries, 859-824-4444.

3. Story told in Lester Sumrall, *60 Things God Said About Sex* (New Kensington, PA: Whitaker House, 1981), 12.

4. Augustine, "Against Two Letters of the Pelagians," 1.34–35.387–88.

5. Sumrall, *60 Things God Said About Sex*, 13–14.

6. Ibid.

7. Ibid.

8. Linda Dillow and Lorraine Pintus, *Intimate Issues: Conversations Woman to Woman* (Colorado Springs: Waterbrook Press, 1999). There is also a Web site, "Intimate Issues," at http://www.intimateissues.com.

9. Ibid., 92–93.

10. Elizabeth Maring (former elder at Willow Creek Community Church), "Defining Moments: Women in Leadership," audio discussion, Willow Creek Association, 2004.

Chapter 13: Wise Boundaries and Fences

Epigraph. William Reddick, "Standin' in de Need o' Prayer" (New York: Huntzinger & Dilworth, 1918).

1. Henry Rogers, *The Silent War: Ministering to Those Trapped in the Deception of Pornography* (Green Forest, AR: New Leaf Press, 2000).

2. Personal e-mail from John Ortberg to the authors, July 2006.

3. Jill Bremer, quoted in "Touch Points" by Tara Weiss (August 2006), http://jobs.aol.com/article/_a/touch-points/20060803163409990001.

Chapter 14: Modesty: Exalting the New Taboo

Epigraph. Jack Benny, quoted in Mardy Grothe, *Oxymoronica: Paradoxical Wit and Wisdom from History's Greatest Wordsmiths* (New York: HarperCollins, 2004), 25.

Epigraph. Dannah Gresh, *Secret Keeper: The Delicate Power of Modesty* (Chicago: Moody, 2002), 11.

1. Internet Movie Database, "Trivia for 'I Dream of Jeannie,'" http://www.imdb.com/title/tt0058815/trivia.

2. Wendy Shalit, *A Return to Modesty: Discovering the Lost Virtue* (New York: Free Press, 1999), 62.

3. Joan Jacobs Brumberg, *The Body Project: An Intimate History of American Girls* (New York: Random House, 1998), xxi–xxii.
4. James S. Spiegel, *How to Be Good in a World Gone Bad: Living a Life of Christian Virtue* (Grand Rapids: Kregel, 2004), 137.
5. Ibid.
6. Naomi Wolf, "The Porn Myth," *New York*, October 20, 2003. This article is also available online at http://nymag.com/nymetro/news/trends/n_9437/.
7. Spiegel, *How to Be Good in a World Gone Bad*, 140.

Chapter 15: Pornography

Epigraph. Neil T. Anderson, *The Bondage Breaker: Overcoming Negative Thoughts, Irrational Feelings, and Habitual Sins* (Eugene, OR: Harvest House, 1990).
1. "The *Leadership* Survey on Pastors and Internet Pornography," *Leadership Journal* 22, no. 1 (Winter 2001).
2. Jason Lee Miller, "Sale of sex.com breaks records," WebProNews.com (January 25, 2006), http://www.webpronews.com/topnews/2006/01/25/sale-of-sexcom-breaks-records.
3. National Coalition for the Protection of Children and Families at http://www.nationalcoaltion.org.

Chapter 16: Safeguards for Spouses

Epigraph. Helen Rowland, quoted in Bob Kelly, *Worth Repeating* (Grand Rapids: Kregel, 2003), 223.
Epigraph. Rodney Dangerfield, as quoted on BrainyQuote.com, http://www.brainyquote.com/quotes/quotes/r/rodneydang154018.html.
1. Bill Hybels, "Defining Moments: Women in Leadership," audio discussion, Willow Creek Association, 2004.
2. George Barna, "Women Are the Backbone of the Christian Congregations in America," *The Barna Update*, March 6, 2000. This article can be found online at http://www.barna.org/FlexPage.aspx?Page=BarnaUpdate&BarnaUpdateID=47.

Scripture Index

Subject Index

adelphoi, 81
aggression, 118–21
Allender, Dan, 44, 66, 79, 83, 83–84, 99, 110, 131, 219
Anderson, Neil, 212
Antioch church, leadership team of, 89–90
apostle, 242n. 13
Aquila, 54–55
assertiveness, 118, 121–22
Augustine, 100, 178

Babette's Feast, 41
Baker, Joye, 27–28
Benny, Jack, 202
Bock, Darrell, 250n. 2
Bremer, Jill, 196
Brown, Dan, 51
Brumberg, Joan Jacobs, 204–5

Carmichael, Amy, 76
celibacy, 178
church in America, decline of, 28–29

Dallas Theological Seminary, 27–28
Dangerfield, Rodney, 221
DaVinci Code, The (Brown), 51
diakonon, 52
Dillow, Linda, 178–79
Dio Chrysostom, 156
Dugdale, Pamela, 63

East of Eden (Steinbeck), 72
Edwards, Sue, 22–23, 43, 79–80, 85–86, 88, 91, 95–96, 119–20, 121, 122, 123, 124, 127–28, 128, 129–30, 161–62, 180–82, 186, 187
Elliot, Elisabeth, 55
Engelthaler, Lesa, 107–8
Epimenides, 58
ethos, 66; biological family ethos, 77; church ethos, 76–77; family ethos, 81–85 (*see also* "one another" phrases in the New Testament); impact of leaders on, 78–79; invisible influence

257

Merrill, William P., 133
Miller, Dianne, 128
Miller, Ronna, 66, 114–15
ministry models: the business/
    professional model, 80–81;
    the family model, 81–85; the
    military model, 79–80
mixed-gender team "rules" for
    brothers: drop demeaning
    language, 140–41; invite
    sisters into the conversation,
    143–44; recognize the benefits
    of women in ministry, 134–38;
    speak up for sisters, 144;
    understand that women feel
    a difference, 139–40; value
    sisters' contributions, 141–42;
    work with the differences,
    142–43
mixed-gender team "rules" for
    sisters: be like the women who
    stood by Jesus, 125–27; choose
    your battles carefully, 123–24;
    develop relationships with
    your brothers' families, 128;
    develop a servant's heart, 118;
    don't bash your brothers, 128–
    29; encourage your brothers
    with appropriate words, 129–
    31; enter your brothers' world,
    128; pray for brothers and
    their families, 127–28; pursue
    emotional health, 127; speak
    up in grace and with wisdom,
    113–23; walk the line, 124–25
Möbius, Paul Julius, 104
modesty, 153–53, 206; biblical
    perspective on, 206–7; lack of
    in American culture, 204–5;
    in the way we dress, 208–11
mutual assignments as siblings in
    Christ, 108: life's tasks, 109;
    obedience, 109–10; salvation,
    108; sanctification, 109;
    service, 110

"one another" phrases in the
    New Testament: "accept one
    another," 89–91; "be devoted to
    one another," 85; "[bear] with
    one another in love," 91–92;
    "encourage one another," 85–
    86; "greet one another," 86–87;
    "serve one another," 87–88
Origen, 153
Ortberg, John, 28, 144, 191, 239n. 7

Pagels, Elaine, 51
patronization, 79, 140
Paul as a model brother, 61–62;
    with sisters in Crete, 58–61;
    with sisters in Philippi, 56–57;
    with sisters in Rome, 52–56
Penn, Michael Philip, 244n. 5
Peterson, Eugene, 171, 250n. 5
Phoebe, 52–53
Pintus, Lorraine, 178–79
pornography, 154, 213–14; counting
    the cost of involvement in,
    218; influence of on men's
    view of women, 218–220; and
    the Internet, 214–15; practical
    ideas for avoiding it, 217; as a
    progressive trap, 214
Priscilla, 53–55
prostates, 53

Quine, Jay, 30, 240n. 12

Reddick, William, 188
Regarding the Physiological Weak-
    Mindedness of Women (Möbius),
    104
Return to Modesty, A (Shalit), 204
Robinson, Haddon, 87, 128
Roese, Steve, 81, 124–25, 134–35,
    140, 144, 183
Rogers, Henry J., 141–42, 143,
    172, 188–89; boundaries and
    fences constructed by, 192–98
Rowland, Helen, 221

Santayana, George, 135
Sax, Leonard, 103, 105, 128–29
Sex and Cognition (Kimura), 102
sexual sin: the church's hiding of,
    157–58; Jesus' dealing with
    sexual sin, 158, 163–70; the
    steps to sexual sin (attraction,
    deliberation, consummation),
    182–86; strategies for dealing
    with, 158–60
sexual temptation, 25–26, 150; and
    sexual attraction, 175–80. *See
    also* pornography
sexual temptation, Christian
    principles for dealing with:
    be careful with compliments,
    195–96; be on guard, 198;
    don't discuss your marital
    problems with members of the
    opposite sex, 192; don't make
    insulting or impractical rules,
    197–98; don't put yourself
    in compromising positions,
    193, 194, 195; flee from it,
    215–16; maintain an open
    profession of faith, 197; make
    sure touching is appropriate,
    196–97; make your marriage
    a priority, 192–93; nurture
    sound mental/emotional
    health, 199–201; when
    looking, follow the three-
    second rule, 194
sexual temptation, ministry
    organizations dealing with,
    250n. 2
sexual temptation, protection
    from, 30, 154, 186–87;
    need for church strategies
    regarding, 156–60; Ortberg's
    three tests (Sibling Test,
    Screen Text, Secret Test),
    191, 194, 196; the uselessness
    of a strategy of isolation/

segregation, 28, 30, 151–53.
    See also sexual temptation,
    Christian principles for
    dealing with
Shalit, Wendy, 204
siblings, biological, 63–64, 67; as
    allies, 68–69; and conflict
    management, 72; as helpers,
    69–70; and insight, 71; as
    protectors, 67; and unity,
    72–73
siblings in Christ, 25, 64–67,
    84, 108; as allies, 69; and
    appropriate attire, 209; biblical
    perspective on, 26–27, 31; and
    conflict management, 72; as
    helpers, 70; and insight, 71; as
    protectors, 67–68; and sibling
    rivalry, 25; and unity, 73–74.
    See also Jesus as a model brother;
    mixed-gender team "rules"
    for brothers; mixed gender
    team "rules" for sisters; mutual
    assignments as siblings in
    Christ; Paul as a model brother
Simon (Niger), 90
Simpsons, The, 101–2
Sister Sledge, 112
Spiegel, James S., 206, 210
spouses, safeguarding of, 155;
    address the issue of attraction,
    227–28; communicate clearly
    and frequently, 225–26; get
    help from trusted outside
    parties, 228; seek emotional
    health above success, 229
Stonehouse, Scott, 129, 153, 193
Sumner, Sarah, 64, 65

Taff, Russ, 21
Talbot, Kristen, 23–24
Tertullian, 100, 153
Thames, Jim, 32, 240n. 13
Tutu, Desmond, 149

THE SUE EDWARDS INDUCTIVE BIBLE STUDY SERIES

Sue Edwards's Bible studies provide women with resources for enriching personal Bible study and meaningful group discussion as they explore the valuable truths and encouragement found throughout Scripture.

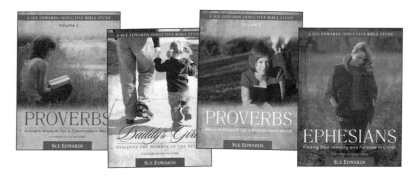

"*Daddy's Girls* enabled me to identify ways in which my relationship with my earthly father impacted my understanding of God."

—DR. JOYE BAKER
Adjunct Professor of Christian Education
Dallas Theological Seminary

"This study of everyday wisdom from Proverbs drew the women back each week with an excitement we had not seen before. Life-changing convictions became the norm as we worked through the material together."

—BARBARA NEUMANN
Director of Ministry to Women
Grace Community Bible Church
Richmond, Texas

"We are presently studying Ephesians and loving it! It has been wonderful to keep everyone united on the same track, when we came from so many different tracks."

—DR. PHYLLIS BENNETT
Director of Women's Ministries
Grace Baptist Church
Hudson, Massachusetts

SUCCESSFUL MINISTRY TO WOMEN

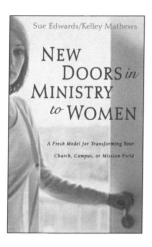

A successful women's ministry is fundamental to the health of any church. This book offers an exciting new strategy—the Transformation Model—that adapts to and addresses the needs of women unique to the postmodern church, ensuring a vital ministry.

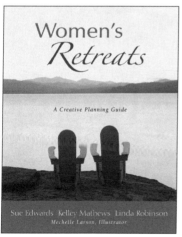

This workbook will guide leaders through a fresh, practical approach to planning and implementing transforming retreats for women. It offers a month-by-month checklist as well as detailed examples of successful retreats that any church can borrow or adapt.

Kregel
Publications